WRITTEN BY

12 INSPIRING AUTHORS

# Letters of Love

*TO NAZY,*

*MAY THIS BOOK BRING YOU
HOPE AND INSPIRATION.
LOVE & LIGHT,*

*VERONICA*

PUBLISHED BY MELISSA DESVEAUX

# Letters of Love

## A collection of Uplifting Written Letters From Around the World

© 2021 - Melissa Desveaux

Published in Australia by Melissa Desveaux Consulting

ISBN – 978-0-9924993-9-6

Cover photo - Diana Akhmetianova, dreamcraftlove@gmail.com
Editing - Jody E Freeman
Cover design - Melissa Desveaux
Illustrations - Damien Desveaux
Photos- pages 19, 26  - SarahMeiPhotography .com

For bulk orders, contact:
melissa@melissadesveauxconsulting.com

www.Melissadesveauxconsulting.com

# Dedication

To our family, friends and the one's we love, this book is
dedicated to you

To bring you joy, inspiration and love

To show you that we care and thank you for your
love and support

So you know that we are grateful to have
you in our lives

Because we wouldn't be who we are today without you

And to tell you, we LOVE you

# Epigraph Of Love

"**Love** is patient and kind;

Love does not envy or boast; it is not arrogant or rude. It does not insist on its own way; it is not irritable or resentful; it does not rejoice at wrongdoing , but rejoices with truth"
1 Corinthians 13:4-6

**Fear** says "I *can't*"

Love says "YES *you can*"

Fear says "O*n my own, it's lonely out here*"

Love says, "Y*ou have a tribe, find each other.*"

Fear says "M*aybe tomorrow, next year...*"

Love says "N*ow*"

Fear says "I *am not ready*"

Love says "W*ell, I'm ready for both of us*"

Fear says "Y*ou can't do it*"

Love says "Y*ou did it*!!!"

Who do you listen to???

I *choose faith, hope and* LOVE.

**LOVE WINS!**

- Libby Monica

# SONNET XVII

From One Hundred Love Sonnets by Nobel Prize Poet Pablo Neruda

I do not love you as if you were salt-rose, or topaz,

or the arrow of the carnations the fire shoots off.

I love you as certain dark things are to be loved, in secret, between the shadow and the soul.

I love you as the plant that never blooms but carries in itself the light of hidden flowers; thanks to your love a certain solid fragrance, risen from the earth, lives darkly in my body.

I love you without knowing how, or when, or from where. I love you directly, without complexities or pride; so I love you because I know no other way than this: where I does not exist, nor you, so close that your hand on my chest is my hand, so close that your eyes close as I fall asleep.

\*\*\*

Thats what people who love you do,

They put their arms around you and love you

when you're not so loveable

- Deb Caletti

# Reviews

"I absolutely love Veronica's letter.
I think it is exactly what we need, especially in times like these.
It makes you realise what are the important things in life, how to cherish them and appreciate them. The secret is in love and appreciation."

- Anna Yaramboykova
CEO Kicks Academy Professional Development LTD- London, UK

\*\*\*

"Rebekah's letter of love touched my heart like no other. Not just because she speaks from a place of deep understanding but because she so directly speaks to MY heart in her words.  It brings what the world believes love to be into the light and shares who love is."

- Carole Jean Whittington
Mind Your Autistic Brain with Social Autie

\*\*\*

"Sarah's letter is moving and inspirational. After going through such unimaginable loss, it is a testament to her strength that she continues to create a lasting legacy to Jasper. Sarah's letter offers a different perspective on grief and how we change after a person we love is gone."

- Rhiannon Koch

"A meaningful, heartwarming letter written to Melissa's son's. It is so raw, loving & thoughtful, I shed tears in my eyes. Just beautiful."

\*\*\*

"A beautiful testimony from a loving son to his beloved mother. Such loving words written for his mum, any mother would be very proud."

Martina Vassallo

\*\*\*

"When reading this beautiful letter, my heart filled with so much love. It shows how much love a mother has for their child. What an amazing and special letter to this writer's sons. Something they will cherish forever. A beautiful read."

Rebecca Riggio

\*\*\*

"This is so relatable! It's as if Rebekah's letter was written for me and for you too! You can tell it's written from the heart with love and meaning. It is such a gift, written with a powerful empowering message. I sat here and cried reading it, it's amazing and I'd recommend it to anyone because
I love it so much!"

Arjaye, Cozy Woodland Cottage Knits

# Contents

# Introduction

We all want to be and feel loved. It's a natural part of who we are. Without love, there is no hope or faith. Without love, there is no happiness.

Letters of Love is a book that shares the secrets to love in all it's different forms. Self-love, love for family, love for the universe, love for God, love for a partner or friend, love for a congregation of people who surround us. Love of life and what we share with others.

We entered 2020 in a worldwide turmoil, and this book will bring some hope, faith, and positivity back into our lives. We will see love differently from the twelve authors who have written their own inspiring letters to the ones they love.

These authors came into my life through the online world and responded to my calling—to share the love. They are all immensely talented in their own ways and very dear to me. People come into our lives for a reason, and we all learn from them. These people have come into my life to make a big impact in the world with me.

I am so proud of these authors for courageously writing their letters. For some, it could not have been easy. They are not ordinary "love letters." They are truly deep and meaningful. Moving and warming. Inspiring and empowering.

I am more than blessed to share these uplifting letters of love from around the world with you.

It fills my heart with joy to see how other people view love and how they show it to the people they care about most.

I am honoured to introduce you to Letters of Love. I hope you read these letters with an open mind and heart and learn from each letter that love comes in many forms.

Thank you to all the authors for contributing to this wonderful book. You have been amazing and I could not have put this together without all your love, support, and encouragement.

I appreciate you all so very much.

With love,

Melissa Desveaux

Author and Publisher

# Authors

Melissa Desveaux

Melysa Aldiano

Naomi Beverly

Willema Girard

Libby Monica

Sarah Pridham

Rebekah Samuel

Veronica Sanchez

Kerri-Ann Sheppard

Abigail Sinclaire

Nor Suhir

David Vine

*"The love between a mother and their child
will forever be tied"*

*"Brothers are for life."*

To my loving boys,

# Damien and Ethan

Since the day you were born, I've been filled with a love I never knew. It's been so beautiful to see you grow into the young boys you are, and I'm so proud of you.

I am writing my letter to you both, so you know how much I love you and so you know that I will always be there for you.

***

## Damien. My DD,

When you came into our lives, I was just so happy you were safe. Our doctor made sure of it even though your birth wasn't how we expected. We were rushed to the operation room because your delivery was an emergency. We could have lost you that day. When I met you for the first time, my heart was filled with so much joy and love. Both your dad and I cried.

Just bringing you into our life wasn't easy. We've told you about your siblings in Heaven who came before and after you—Charlize, your elder sister and three other babies we couldn't meet. All I wanted was to have a beautiful, happy, and healthy baby. God blessed me with you.

It's been fun watching you grow. You are so smart and witty. I'm proud of all your achievements so far, and I know that you can do anything you put your mind to. Please believe that you can, too. Don't ever let anyone tell you otherwise.

Your love for playing the piano, music and singing, your creative mind to compose your own beats on the iPad as well as draw fills my heart with joy. You amaze me every day.

Sometimes I forget that you're still young, probably because your brother is a few years younger, and you're mature for your age. Maybe a little too much sometimes! :)

When you wanted "Da Monkey" (your Build a Bear), it made me realise that you're still a kid, and I'm glad you opened my eyes. I wish you could stay young forever.

The effort you put into your work at school and in everything you do shows me that you really do try hard to be the best you can be. And so do your classmates because they've voted you class captain in each year of school so far!

Try your hardest with everything you do in life. If you want to achieve something, don't hesitate. Listen to your heart. I will do everything I can to support you. You don't need to make me or your dad proud of you. We always are.

Be proud of yourself and love yourself for who you are.

Later in life, you'll read this letter and probably laugh, but here's some truth. Remember these three things in life: Listen. Show Respect. Be Kind.

I know that watching that gamer "Jelly" or "Dan TDM" and all those other YouTubers is fun (for you, not me!) and jumping up and down with the Xbox controller, screaming at your brother while you're playing those games that are too old for you is exciting, but just remember to listen.

Ignoring people comes across as rude and disrespectful. This is not what I expect from you.

When you listen, you show others that you care and that you understand.

Please be respectful and kind to your family, especially your brother, your friends, and the people you meet along your journey through your life. There will be people who may take you for granted or try to hurt you. Some people will come and go, but the ones that will stay are the ones you should keep. You will know who they are.

When you treat people with respect and kindness, you will live a happy life because it will feel good, even if the other person doesn't do the same. When you treat yourself well, you will live an even happier life.

You have a good heart, DD, and I know without a doubt you will do well in all areas of your life.

Just keep learning, love life, listen, show respect, and be kind to others.

If you ever need someone to talk to, I will always listen. I love you more than you know.

*** 

## Ethan. My little EE,

When you were still in my belly, I was so worried something would happen to you while you were growing. When the doctor told me that you may have to be born sooner than we thought, I couldn't think or go through losing another baby.

So the next morning, I waited in a hospital room while the doctor was getting ready to take me into the operation room to deliver you. I spoke to you and said that I was excited to be meeting you soon and that I loved you. I knew then that you would be okay.

When you were born, I gave you a kiss on your head and said hello to you. I was so happy to finally meet you. You completed our family.

Damien was so happy to have a little brother to take care of and he did as you were growing up. He still does now.

You amaze me every day, Ethan. You are so affectionate, smart, and funny. You make me laugh so much! Just like when you used to get so angry you became Hulk or when you make up your own songs, like the one you made up "your beautiful dress" ...  Or when you sing songs in the car and when I turn to look, you tell me to stop. :)

Your teddies are so cute, too. You love them all and like to sleep with them. We make a nest for them, too! Let's see if I can remember their names. There's Myrtle, Tiggi Eye, Billy, Cookie (your Build a Bear),

Choc Chip, and Mr Cheese? I love them all, too.

I love when you give me big hugs and kisses. I hope that your kind and sweet heart stays with you always. Even when you tell your brother you love him, it makes me smile.

You were pretty feisty as a little kid and still are. I remember when you were a baby, you picked up the baby monitor as I was changing your diaper, and you threw it at my eye and it was bruised for a few days so I couldn't go out!

We've had a few scares with you, too. You seem to be the kid that gets hurt, and you've even spent a couple of days in hospital.

You cut your eye and had to get stitches. You broke your leg on a slippery slide while I was holding you. So it was my fault, and I'm sorry. You accidentally swallowed one of my tablets that fell on the floor. The doctors took so many blood tests and had to check for so many infectious diseases. We thought we were going to lose you. That day reminded me of how precious life is.

And then you got an eye infection and we had to stay in hospital again. We watched SpongeBob together and laughed a lot! I stayed up most of the night watching Designated Survivor!

Despite all those incidents, you continue to do well.

You take in everything you learn, from school and of course YouTube, just like your brother. You definitely learn from him, too. You speak so well now and some of the words you say amaze me. You are doing so well in school; reaching your reading goals has made me proud and I know that you are proud, too, because you can read.

Ethan, just remember that you, too, can do anything you choose to in your life if you put your mind to it. Even if you want to become a surgeon so you can save people. I will be there to support you.

Remember to try your hardest to achieve your goals and make yourself proud. It doesn't matter if you don't get something right the first go; just keep practising and learning.

Like I wrote to DD: Listen, be respectful and kind always, and you will be respected by others who come into your life. Even though you are strong and competitive, being stubborn can make you angry, so listen to others before you speak.

Ethan, I enjoy watching you grow bigger and smarter each day, but I wish you could just stay little. Stay who you are, my sweet and caring boy. I love you so much.

***

Damien and Ethan, as brothers, you are sometimes like chalk and cheese although more times than not, you get along so well and you truly do love each other. I hope you stay close as brothers and as friends forever.

I know you will have arguments, especially as you grow, but please forgive each other. As I said, be kind to each other.

As you get older, you'll run into challenges. It's okay. Just take each day as it comes. Stay calm, set goals, and stay focused.

Enjoy your life to the fullest. Explore the world and

learn about different cultures. Meet new people.

Life isn't about what you have. It's about what memories you have and will make and the people you love. Try your best to make good and joyful memories. Take lots of photos, too, so these memories can be shared.

Live a balanced life. Make time for both work and fun. Take care of yourself.

Think of money as energy. The more you give, the more you get back. It can buy you freedom. Keep that in mind and learn how to work smart so you have the freedom to do the things you want and enjoy. Help others in need, give to charity, or volunteer. The rewards are a blessing.

If one day you have a family of your own, be a good partner and father. Please care for them and always be with them when they need you. Enjoy them because they grow way too fast and teach them well. Teach them to also be respectful and kind. Love them more than anything else in the world.

My sons, I hope that you continue to become amazing and grow into loving and caring adults. And don't forget to hug and kiss your mum.

I love you both more than you will ever know and I'm proud to be your mother. I feel that we are doing something right in raising you.

Wishing you both a very happy and fulfilling life.

With love from the bottom of my heart,

Mum

# Melissa Desveaux

Melissa Desveaux is a wife and mother of two boys.

After experiencing the loss of her four babies through miscarriage and stillbirth, she wrote her own memoir, *My Life of Loss*, and has compiled and published two anthologies, *Comfort for the tears, Light for the way* and *Comfort for the Tear*s. These collections are written by women who have also experienced pregnancy struggles.

As well as being featured in a number of publications, one being on the Brainz 500 Global list of 2020, Melissa has also contributed to three other anthologies. Her latest anthology, *Letters of Love*, is written by twelve authors around the world to share love in many forms.

As an author consultant, Melissa took the steps to grow a business helping inspiring authors write and self publish their own personal stories so that they can inspire and change lives.

She has won an Australia Day Award for her dedication and commitment to helping families deal with pregnancy and infant loss and is a Peer Support Ambassador for the Pink Elephants Support Network.

Melissa's children are her driving force and her reason for writing her own letter in *Letters of Love*.

She aims to create a lifestyle that allows for more time to see the world and provide opportunities to learn from new experiences and make many joyful memories with her family.

# Ray of Sunshine Amongst the Storm

In the summer of 1980, high up on a mountain in the middle of the stormy night, in a tropical land called the Philippines, there was a child with golden hair, so tiny and tender and loved in the arms of her mother the moment she was born.

A ray of sunshine she was to everyone she knew and loved by everyone she met. Yet, fate had different plans for her.

That child was me...

It's been too long that you've suffered from anger, or even perhaps hate, that has rooted inside of you beyond your innocent understanding, unconsciously. A rage built throughout your entire childhood. That trait has impacted your well-being in all aspects of your life.

Now, this is the time to let go of all the hurts and brokenness inside you. It is time to confront that little hurt girl and heal your broken heart. This is the reason why I write this letter to you, my younger self, "Melysa."

\*\*\*

My dearest "Melysa,"

You were always different from the crowd, not only because you were born less financially fortunate, but rather for standing up for yourself at a young age despite having an innocent yet curious mind. You've always followed your intuition no matter how frightened you were, a strong instinct that has guided you throughout the years of trials and struggles.

Indisputably, how could you understand that those hurdles you have been through in the past were the best life lessons that became the catalysts of who and what you have become today?

Do you still remember the time when you were four years old that Father taught you how to ride a bicycle? The bicycle was so huge you could barely touch the ground with your feet! But it didn't matter to you; you were so happy and proud of learning how to ride your oversize bicycle.

Because you were having fun, your heart was overjoyed that you'd achieved something so little that still had significant meaning to you. You have to admit that it was one of the most beautiful moments you shared with your father.

I do still remember as if it was yesterday. It is a moment I will treasure forever.

Little did you know, those candid moments only stay for a while.

You grew up in an environment where you have not seen a divine example from your father, but rather witnessed abusive drinking, gambling, adulteries, betrayals and painful situations he caused you and your entire family.

However, as of today looking from my perspective, an older and wiser "Melysa," I can say that you are still so lucky having a mother who taught you everything that is good and wonderful about life: Carrying the faith toward God. Having an attitude of integrity. Being utterly honest with yourself.

And simply, a mother who guided you to become the independent young lady you are despite everything that has occurred and you witnessed from your father. You have gained and built a joyful heart regardless of the cruel environment! For that alone, I have come to realize that those obstacles have not only shaped you but pushed you to move forward, and seek answers in life for a greater cause...

I want to assure you, my dearest "Melysa," that you were so lucky to have received the unconditional love from your grandfather who believed in you. He taught you to be proud of who you are! He taught you karate and kickboxing, taught you to drive, went fishing for you when you were just a baby so that you had delicious food on your plate. He guided you all the way and stood up for you at all times against everybody when no one was listening. He became your father figure and an example of what a father should be to their children and taught you to laugh and be the light that you are.

And oh, I miss him so dearly. I wish I could call him today and say "thank you" for being our guardian angel...

You were granted multiple talents such as dancing, singing, a creative mind in all platforms, and leadership that landed you in different spaces in your childhood; always one of the best in the crowd. Once again, all these, despite the rejection from your father who irrefutably showed and said to you, "Education is not necessary, let alone sending you to prominent schools and university!" However, all of these things happened through the guidance of your mother who worked hard for you and your younger siblings and provided everything the best she could.

In the midst of all the hardships you've witnessed as a young child and the countless rejections, especially from your father, you've always managed to bear a joyful smile, so contagious that everyone wants to be surrounded by you. You have pure and genuine happiness in your heart. Those are traits that you inevitably couldn't hide from the world because no matter how hard things were back then or might seem to you or how impossible it may look like, where there life is, there is hope.

Certainly, at that time you couldn't tell, but I tell you now that since you were born, you've perpetually brought happiness and joy to many. That is because you have a pure heart infused with love.

Many would have repeatedly said to you that you bring light once you enter the room, and you never understood why. This is a God-given gift you cannot disregard, a gift that you later used to impact lives! Leave a significant legacy to your future children and theirs.

Show humanity that you are not what happened to you. You are what you choose to become! Your past does not define who you are today!

All these I want to share with you because I know you asked yourself for too long, "Why did certain things occur in my life that seemed so painful and mostly unfair?" I don't blame you for that, but as mentioned earlier, fear not. All the past pains and obstacles you've encountered were the best life lessons you could ever have. The best experiences in life will be the catalysts of who and what you will become in your future self.

If I knew back then what I know now...

In spite, you've questioned God's work. He was always watching over you and still does.

There was this one event in your life that turned you to an adult overnight when you were just eight years old. You stood up for your seven-months pregnant mother. Your drunk, abusive father carried an axe and almost threw it at you and your mother! In this situation alone, if God wasn't watching over you, you could have possibly been hurt badly, or even worse, it could have been your death. But instead, God protected you.

You were captive with anxieties, crying while holding a broomstick, carrying the thought that it would protect your mother. Your body was shaking, mind disoriented, and you almost went into shock! Inside, you were screaming and asking for help! Then your grandfather came to rescue you both and took the axe. That, "Melysa," was God's work. From that moment on, you bore the responsibility of protecting your mother at all costs, unconsciously.

There were countless moments like these that you have questioned why certain things in your life happened. Still, you haven't lost hope in life. Instead, you kept moving forward. You've always seen the good things in life. All these are irrefutable truths of God's way of saying, "I got your back," surrender all your worries and I will guide you through."

One thing is certain. I want you to remember, no matter how messy or uncomfortable it might seem to you. Trust the process. Surrender every worry you have.

As this Biblical phrase from Matthew 7:7-8 says: *"Ask, and it will be given to you; seek, and you will find; knock, and it will be opened to you. For everyone who asks receives, and the one who seeks finds, and to the one who knocks, it will be opened."*

Nobody is spared from adversity in life as we know it. However, I want to assure you that all the occurrences in your life happened for a reason, for a greater cause you aren't fully aware of it yet ... and that you, "Melysa," are meant to create an impact not merely to your surroundings, but rather to your legacy and theirs.

Share your story with the world and show them how your journey in all walks of life throughout the years, with ups and downs, all go back to one thing only, and that was always your belief and trust in God. Carry the faith that has been rooted inside you ever since you were little.

As Maya Angelou said: "Love recognizes no barriers, it jumps walls to arrive at its destination full of hope." This reminds me of you, and this has guided you in every part and aspect of your life and certainly will in your future.

Let me share the wisdom I learned with you...

*Listen with your heart to Isaiah 9:2: "The people who were walking in darkness have seen a great light. As for those who dwell in the land of deep shadow, light has shone on them."*

Wherever you are in darkness now, whatever agony

your heart carries now or even in the past; perhaps, you have found yourself where it is hard to have hope, hard to believe the peace and love that God promises, hard to feel the joy and happiness you are longing for ... just remember to look out for glimmers of hope in the shadows.

No matter how you feel, you are seen, known, and loved...

Put God as the center of your life. He is capable of all the impossible! Without Him, we are nothing.

Everything you speak of comes to life...

# Melysa Aldiano

Melysa Aldiano was born and raised in Laguna, Philippines. She attended The Polytechnic University in Santa Cruz, Laguna where she studied Bachelor Science of Industrial Technology mastering Electronics Engineering.

In 1998, Melysa move to Austria where she lived for almost a decade and laid another foundation of her life. In 2006, she moved to Belgium where she now lives a happy and joyful life with her two beautiful children, Daniel and Aurora-Victoria, and life-partner Marc.

Melysa loves learning languages , reading and mindfulness. Her passions in her spare time include dance and music. She is an adventurer, outside person, and free spirit.

Melysa is an influencer, a thought leader, an entrepreneur, an International Best-selling author, and a speaker.

Facebook: Melysa Aldiano
Facebook Page: JOY UNFILTERED MOVEMENT
https://www.facebook.com/joyunfilteredmovement/
Instagram: @joy_unfiltered
E-mail: aldianomelysa@gmail.com
Melysa Aldiano – Consulting & Coaching

## To My Dear Children

# James, Sean, SeanaJames, and JaSean,

The words in my vocabulary cannot express how much you all have completely changed my life for the better. Children are not supposed to be born with a job to do, but you each have done a great job keeping me grounded, focused, and pushing me to excel for all of our benefits. Being your mother and your mom has been quite the journey... tough and challenging at times, and SO MUCH FREAKING FUN at others, but every second is so worth it!

I cannot imagine my life without you, even though y'all know that sometimes I imagine what my empty nest will look and feel like once you are gone. I miss quiet, organization, and waking up to find all of my food, treats, and goodies where I left them and in the amounts that I left them.

Still, I love you more than you will ever know, and this letter is my attempt to demonstrate via written word how important, magnificent, special, and valuable you are to me. Simply put ... I LOVE YOU so much. Thank you for choosing me to be your mommy. I work really hard to do the best job possible, and we all know that I reach out for help when it gets overwhelming or when I need to learn new skills to keep up with your new developmental milestones.

We are planning to do a lot of traveling all over the world as soon as it is safe. With that said, you know how much I stress learning about and understanding other cultures, perspectives, ways of living, and religions or belief systems as an act of love. Throughout this letter, you'll see me reference our main belief systems and foundations—universal law and Christ consciousness—while acknowledging the timeless wisdom and interconnected themes of love found in other systems of beliefs.

Because love is everywhere; all around us, inside of us, and in unlimited quantities no matter where we find ourselves. Spend your time learning how to love and seeking it out. Vibrate at that frequency. It's all you need to have a successful life, in my humble opinion. Remember who you are, love yourself, and to extend that love to others.

That's it. Everything else is an extension of these ideas.

But what IS love, really?

Throughout your life, you'll meet people who will try to convince you that THEIR way is the ONLY way and their understanding is THE ONLY understanding that you should have, or that their path is THE ONLY path you should take. They'll just ambush you sometimes, inexplicably, out of nowhere and try to force their opinions on you in the name of "love." Or, they'll try to convince you that if you do not believe what they think, you are wrong, going to "hell," or will miss out on going to "heaven."

I find that extremely condescending, manipulative, and aggressive.

Children of mine, pay them no attention. Smile and nod, then move on. Additionally, I suggest that you protect your peace by rejecting that energy and send it back into the atmosphere from which it came. With love, of course. To me, behavior such as that is not love at all. It's ego, pride, and conceit wrapped in a thin, translucent veneer painted with the word "love" on the outside.

Beloveds, as your mom, I encourage you to seek answers within yourself. I want you to know that love DOES NOT shove itself down your throat. It's not going to present itself as a pushy salesman would, pressing on your pain points and feeding into your fears, vulnerabilities, and traumas.

Love is not rooted in the fear of missing out: FOMO. Love offers itself. It's gentle and feels good. It's sweet and humble. True love feels so good that you will seek out the Divinely created love situations meant for you—intuitively. Strengthen your intuition, listen to your intuition, and trust your intuition. Honor your feelings. Those are forms of love.

From what I understand, there are spiritual laws; some of them are immutable while others are mutable. They are the laws of Divine oneness, vibration, attraction, action, correspondence, cause and effect, compensation, perpetual transmutation of energy, gestation/divine timing, polarity, rhythm, belief, and gender. Understanding these laws and applying them to your life, my starseeds, is an act of love. So, start here and study up!

The rest of this letter is a reminder that no matter where you find yourself physically, if you are operating from a place of spiritual love, you are connecting to and tapping into the SOURCE from which all flows. You are operating from a position of power. And that is exactly where you want to be. Enveloped in the power of LOVE.

The Christian canon, 1 Corinthians 13 (verses 1-13) says that:

*"If I speak in the tongues of men or of angels, but do not have love, I am only a resounding gong or a clanging cymbal. If I have the gift of prophecy and can fathom all mysteries and all knowledge, and if I have a faith that can move mountains, but does not have love, I am nothing. If I give all I possess to the poor and give over my body to hardship that I may boast, but do not have love, I gain nothing.*

*Love is patient, love is kind. It does not envy, it does not boast, it is not proud. It does not dishonor others, it is not self-seeking, it is not easily angered, it keeps no record of wrongs. Love does not delight in evil but rejoices with the truth. It always protects, always trusts, always hopes, always perseveres.*

*Love never fails. But where there are prophecies, they will cease; where there are tongues, they will be stilled; where there is knowledge, it will pass away. For we know in part and we prophesy in part, but when completeness comes, what is in part disappears. When I was a child, I talked like a child, I thought like a child, I reasoned like a child. When I became a man, I put the ways of childhood behind me. For now, we see only a reflection as in a mirror; then we shall see face to face. Now I know in part; then I shall know fully, even as I am fully known.*

*And now these three remain: faith, hope and love. But the greatest of these is love."*

There are many times when I have failed to love you, according to these words. And for that, I apologize. I am human, and I make mistakes. I know that I will never be perfect, but I also know that I will always give you my best and continue to make this kind of love my goal.

When it is safe again, we'll travel the world, sharing our gifts, having fun ... and loving others.

When we visit India, we will meet people who believe deeply in Hinduism. Their dharma, or way of life, includes studying the Vedas. One Vedic quote on love is:

*"Those in whose hearts OM reverberates*

*Unceasingly are indeed blessed*

*And deeply loved as one who is the Self.*

*The all-knowing Self was never born,*

*Nor will it die. Beyond cause and effect,*

*This Self is eternal and immutable.*

*When the body dies, the Self does not die."*

*(Katha Upanishad)*

They, too, understand universal love. We are interconnected and the power of Source is within us.

Jainism is a belief system, also from India, that means "path of victory." Their sacred scriptures, the Agamas, teach the supreme principle of non-violence *(ahimsa)*. Concern for all beings is paramount.

I believe that loving yourself is also a radical act of non-violence. When we do not love ourselves, we create situations that reflect our inner state. Things just feel "wrong" and the synchronicity and magic that living in love bring lessens and sometimes comes to a halt. Pay attention to these signs. Discover where you are not being loving, correct it, and then rejoin your path.

When we visit China, we'll meet staunch proponents of Confucianism, a belief system founded by K'ung Fu-Tzu (Confucius) whose sacred text Lun Yu (Analects) places emphasis on moral virtues of humaneness, love *(jen)* and filiality *(hsiao)*. No matter where you go, children ... seek out those who vibrate at the frequency of love.

During the same time that Confucius was sharing his thoughts, Chinese philosopher Mo Tzu said, *"This is true even among thieves and robbers. As he loves only his own family and not other families, the thief steals from other families to profit his own family. As he loves only his own person and not others, the robber does violence to others to profit himself.*

*And the reason for all this is want of love. This again is true in the mutual disturbance among the houses of the ministers and the mutual invasions among the states of the feudal lords. As he loves only his own house and not the others, the minister disturbs the other houses to profit his own. As he loves only his own state and not the others, the feudal lord attacks the other states to profit his own. These instances exhaust the confusion in the world. And when we look into the causes we find they all arise from want of mutual love."* — Mei 19.

Moral? My children, remember to love your neighbors as yourself. Everywhere you go.

As we travel through Thailand and Japan, we'll meet those who believe in Buddhism. The Buddha teaches that the foundation for all spiritual practice is love. Unconditional love that knows no boundaries, to be specific. Because you are all loving and giving, we will fit in well here.

Other regions have their beliefs and of course, the Great Mama Africa has a history full of social practices that demonstrate love as a way of life. Our sisters and brothers in Ghana, Nigeria, and the Ivory Coast will share with us their traditional belief systems. We will listen, learn, take what resonates, and lovingly release what does not serve us.

My loves, thank you again for the privilege and honor of being your mom. I can't wait to travel the world with you, doing what we love while being, giving, and receiving love. Everyday gets better than the day before. Every day, we are increasing our capacity to love ourselves and each other. Every day, we deepen our knowledge of love and practice what we haven't yet mastered.

We will never be perfect, but our promise to each other is to keep trying. It's the effort that sustains us; it's grace that puts us back together again when things fall apart. You four, more than any person or experience that I have encountered, have demonstrated love in its purest form. Thank you for that gift. It's your presence and your love that gives my life purpose.

Your loving mother,

Naomi

XO

# Naomi Beverly

Naomi Beverly is a transformational coach, #1 International Bestselling Author, Publisher, Mental Health Peer Support Specialist, Educator, and Singer from the United States of America.

Her company, Naomi Beverly Coaching, LLC, helps people rebuild their lives after trauma in a supportive community using self-publishing for self-care plus other tools and strategies. Her favorite types of books are those dealing with Social Emotional Learning and Awareness. She holds an M.A. in Education and is one capstone away from an M.Ed in Instructional Design.

During her free time, she enjoys dancing, yoga, meditation, working out, eating well, and being in nature. Naomi is the mother of four amazing children, two of whom have self-published.

You can contact her via email at: naomi@naomibeverlycoaching.com

Schedule a 15-minute discovery Zoom at: https://calendly.com/coachnaomi

Book sessions at www.naomibeverlycoaching.com

Join her Facebook Community "Trauma Survivors: Self-publishing as self-care" at http://www.facebook.com/groups/selfpublishselfcare

Purchase the bestselling book collaboration Birth (Volume II): Stories of Birth, Renewal, and Birthing a New Earth https://amzn.to/38My2kS

# My Dearest Friend

Speaking of love is not always easy. It exposes us and very often, we believe it weakens us. But this is not the case. On the contrary, it makes us much stronger and binds us together.

Today, I am taking the opportunity offered to me to open my heart before it is too late to express my affection for you.

To you who gave me life. You left me too early, even as I was discovering the world. However, I know that in the shadows you watch over me. I love you, Mum.

To you who, in a few years, may not recognize me anymore. We have grown apart, lost touch, but despite our differences, we found each other again. I love you, Dad.

To those who carried me, supported me throughout the years without expecting anything in return. I love you.

And finally, to you who, without knowing or without recognizing it, were there for me. I thank you.

Often people ask me where I get my strength from despite the obstacles life has thrown at me and the medical issues.

"Please tell me, how do you find the strength to

forgive, the will to move forwards, and the optimism to continue to dream of a better world, as well as the energy to commit to it?"


I have thought about it a lot, and I think it is thanks to Love. An unconditional Love which is manifested in different forms.

Whatever our origin, Love binds us together without distinction of race, colour, age, or sex.

Love can be difficult to see or perceive, and/or recognize as it is subtle. Nevertheless, if we take our time, if we watch carefully, there is always something around us to remind us of its presence.

Whether it is in a child's or a stranger's smile, the brushing of a cat, the caress of the sun, or the kiss of a lover. It can also surprise us, at a crossroads, in a surprising encounter or through small gestures, like when someone holds a door open for you, or holds back the elevator for you! We are never alone.

Let's open our eyes, keep our ears open, and pay attention! The universe is speaking to us!

Always present.

For me, Love manifested itself as a mother and a sister. When I was a little girl, they would reassure me, cradle me, and take care of me while I was ill or scared of the dark.

I also recognized it through my friends' attentions and from strangers who, all through the years, encouraged me and trusted me, even in my craziest adventures!

And finally, it was there throughout illness, on the brink of death, as the medical teams fought with me to keep me alive and supported me through rehabilitation processes, and still to this date.

Despite being separated by continents and/or by the daily routine, our relationship remains steadfast and timeless. It is a bit like when a game of chess is started, then interrupted for a short or long period of time. The pawns remain on the chessboard. The game is picked up where it was left off when the players are reunited as if nothing had happened.

I remember this night when we were on call at the hospital, exhausted after these four nights and you told me you would always be there for me. I don't think either of us thought it would happen!I do not think you know what you were committing to. Yet, you have never disappointed me. On the contrary, you have often surprised me like when you jumped on a plane from the other side of the world to come to see me, to support me as I was drowning in the twists and turns of life and financial difficulty.

I also remember you who took me under your wing upon my arrival in the university and you who snubbed me. Nothing predestined us to be friends and yet we have had many adventures together! Here we are, twenty years later, with lots of memories to share and more to come!

And finally, you, who are called "homeless" (sans-domicile-fixe, or SDF in French), who no one turns around for. And yet, you saved me, protected me, fed me when I was terrified and forgotten in a train station, late at night and with no money, didn't know where to turn. I would never have thought you could help me in this way and guide me to the light.

Rich, poor, famous or unknown, single, married or divorced, ill or in good health, from here or from elsewhere, always present for one another!

Very often doors have closed in front of me. I have been underestimated or told that it was not for me, or I would not succeed. I have had many knock-backs, I have been disappointed, betrayed, and I was often scared. I did not know where I was going nor what I should do. But you have always been there for me in one way or another. Even in my darkest hours, at the trough of the wave, you listened to me, encouraged me, took care of my well-being (either by text message, a phone call, a note, a smile…).

All these little and big nothings have carried me. All these small moments and souvenirs fill my heart and my being with warmth, and when I am thinking of them, they bring tears to my eyes. Happiness!

I do not know what life has in store for me, but I take with me all your loving and all your attentions. I am sharing them every day with the world and anyone I meet.

I may not have told you before because it was not in my nature to say these things! But please know that I love you for having loved me so without judgement and for being present in my life.

Tenderly, Willema

# Willema Girard

Founder and CEO of Reveal3

Founder and Chairwoman of RFWB Association

Certified Executive Master Coach: Critical Incident, Stress Management, Leadership Development

Certified Mental Health First Aid

True believer in 2030 SDGs Actions – Humanitarian – People Voice

Born in Guadeloupe (French Caribbean Island), living in Switzerland

Contact :

email: willema.girard@reveal-3.com / contact@rfwb-association.org

website: https://reveal-3.com/home/

LinkedIn: linkedin.com/in/wgirard

My Dearest Mum, Clemencia,

# This is a precious moment in time

You and I, both alive and living in this world together. Laughing, learning, loving, and each creating their own legacy.

What a perfect moment for me to sit here, in near silence, enjoying the soothing voice of Jim Reeves singing quietly in the background. I am reminded of you and why I still love country music.

Back in the days, the sound of the music was more significant and familiar to me. Today, it is the lyrics that have become more audible as I dedicate this song to you, an old-time favourite of yours, Mum:

*I love you because you understand, dear*

*Every single thing I try to do*

*You're always there to lend a helping hand, dear*

*I love you most of all because you're you.*

*No matter what the world may say about me*

*I know your love will always see me through*

*I love you for the way you never doubt me*

*But most of all I love you 'cause you're you.*

*I love you because my heart is lighter*

*Every time I'm walking by your side*

*I love you because the future's brighter*

*The door to happiness, you open wide.*

*No matter what the world may say about me*

*I know your love will always see me through*

*I love you for a hundred thousand reasons*

*But most of all I love you 'cause you're you.*

The year 2020 has been a testing one for humanity. Whilst many have experienced social distancing and family separation for the first time, I survived yet another year of long-term separation from you and my Zim family.

Thankfully, our long telephone conversations and access to social media take the sting out of the distance. I still remember times before social media and smartphones when the only communication options were "snail mail" and public phone booths that were rather fussy about the size of the coins they accepted!

*Today, I write you a letter*

I am revisiting the old-fashioned practice of letter writing just to tell you how much I love you. I value that I can communicate this love to you. There is a small twist, though. Instead of heading to the post office for an envelope and stamp, I have plucked up courage, won the battle with fear, and taken this opportunity to have this letter to you published. Yes, published!

In addition to influencing one genre of my varied music taste, you also passed on to me a love for reading. The children have a pet tortie and every now and then, I have a private giggle, thinking about my once-upon-a-time favourite, Puss in Boots. I even remember my favourite and significant pair of red, smooth, velvet boots you bought for petite, four-year-old me, vowing, *"I will not let a speck of dirt on these boots!"*

With fairy tales came colouring by numbers, dot to dot art, crossword puzzles, word searches, and finally writing. Writing that started off with the pencil always naturally drawn to my left hand, but with encouragement moved to my right until in the confusion I mastered the art of alternating between the two!

I still enjoy these childhood hobbies which in my adult years have become forms of therapy. Dad (RIP) always looked forward to receiving my letters and loyally replied with compliments about my impressive vocabulary, grammar, and spelling accuracy. I teased him in response, pointing out that the teacher in him had retired but certainly never left!

By the age of fourteen, I knew I wanted to become an author as much as I wanted to one day get married and have children. My specific desire to write was driven by an amazing woman I was closely watching. A woman who carried her responsibilities within family and community diligently, leading with kindness, care, and generosity.

*"One day I am going to write your story, Mum," I promised. "It will inspire and motivate many people and will become a best-seller."*

Words are powerful

*"Speak life. Discipline your tongue because it has the power to build and to destroy,"* you said to us. With this instruction came a strict and non-negotiable house rule that stated, *"No one is allowed negative self-talk or negative language directed at anyone else."* Foul language was a deal-breaker. The three magic phrases, *"please;" "thank you;"* and *"sorry"* mattered, and you regularly reminded us about the impact of these small words on the quality of relationships.

Affirmations are gifts you give sincerely and with these, you instilled in me a confidence that empowers me to get back up whenever life throws a knock-out punch my way. Thank you for your positive parenting. In my own tough situations, I wonder, *How would Mum handle this?* A blessing I do not take for granted is that I still have the option to pick up the phone and ask for your opinion.

Like many people, your life has been a mixed bag. You are a perfectly imperfect spiritual being having a human experience, and you know highs as well as lows. What stands out for me is your graceful composure under all circumstances. Through thick and thin, you walk in gratitude, love, and humility, quietly confident that the sun will shine again.

A few years ago, I was deep in the valley. At my worst point, giving up looked deceivingly attractive. In my weakness, you became all the strength that I needed for my family and you carried our weight and responsibilities. *"Get on your knees and pray,"* you said. *"There is a time for everything. Walk in faith, this too shall pass. I am praying for you."*

I know that you pray for me always. You pray not only for me but for all your children and grandchildren and your petitions shelter us.

My winter finally passed. It is spring now.

in Leo Tolstoy's words, and here I am, writing to you and sharing that story about my mother, which at age fourteen, I promised you I would write. Such is the power of words.

Your grandchildren hear stories about you all the time. Stories about your childhood, your challenges, and the transformation that came with your hard work, perseverance, and faith. I see that they, too, are in their spring, learning, planning, and visualising. They are discovering themselves and in their own time, they will fully blossom.

Indeed, there is a time for everything and a season for every activity under heaven.

Your nest is empty now. It brings me joy when you update me on your latest escapades. The church project you are working on or the next fundraising activity in aid of a community initiative. Dinner functions, car boot sales, library visits, and trips abroad. With no childcare arrangements to juggle, no homework assignments and projects to assist with or family dinners to prepare on time, good health is your best friend, and freedom and time, close allies. Enjoy all three.

I too pray for you, Mum. A simple prayer for your long and healthy life so that you may fully enjoy the fruits of your seed. You have courageously and successfully lived with purpose, driven by your vision to change the narrative into which you were born and build a legacy for your children and generations that follow. Thank you, Mum. Your vision resonates with me and lives on. You are sincerely and deeply loved and appreciated. I wish you joy, happiness, and above all, LOVE.

*I love you and I understand, Mum*

*The things that matter to you,*

*Loving, giving, serving and caring*

*I love you most of all because you're you.*

*No matter what the world may say about You*

*I know you love because He first loved you*

*I love you for the way you walk in steadfast faith*

*But most of all I love you 'cause you're you.*

*I love you because my heart is safe*

*Every time you are walking by my side*

*I love you because the future's brighter*

*The door to limitless possibilities, you opened wide.*

*No matter what the world may say about You*

*I know your love comes from The Fountain of Love*

*I love you for a hundred thousand reasons*

*But most of all I love you 'cause you're you...*

My Children, Rudaviro Clemencia, Runako Anthony, and Joley Mufaro,

# Many times, I have told you that I love you

I will continue to tell you this forever, but it would take an eternity for these words to adequately express the true depth of what I mean. Each one of you is a precious and treasured gift, loved differently but equally. Mothering you is a privilege and there are three moments in my life that I hold most dear.

Rudie, at 01:40am on a calm, warm Tuesday night in the midst of a Zimbabwean summer, you changed my life forever. You opened the door to my childhood dream of becoming a mum, bringing with you the gifts of life-purpose and love. *"Thank you, Baby Girl."*

Five years later, at 07:28am on a cool, crisp Tuesday morning at the start of an Irish spring, you too changed my life forever. I would now know the experience of raising both a daughter and a son. You brought with you the gifts of balance and love. You ground me. *"Thank you, Baby Boy."*

Another four years later, along came the last member of our family, loved by her parents and siblings from the moment she was still an idea. Joley, at 00:30am on a wet, wintry Sunday night, you arrived with bags of love and enough warmth to cancel winter. *"Thank you, Baby Girl."*

Today, I look at all three of you in wonder. Where have the years gone?

## Rudaviro,

*"My Rudie, my own one."*

I admire and respect the beautiful young lady that you have grown to become in nineteen years. An attentive and empathic listener, kind-hearted, caring, gentle, reasonable, and quietly balanced, strong, and determined. We are all so blessed to have you in our family. A third adult opinion for Mum and Dad and a sounding board Runako and Joley.

At an early age, you identified your purpose in life, to help and to heal many. The next six college years will be tough, but you are tougher. Keep going, Doc McRudie, one step at a time. You have a strong team behind you rooting for your success!

I love receiving photos from you, of your latest adventures. Continue to work hard and play harder.   I am excited for your next trip home or maybe a family weekend break this time over at yours? There will be some tea to spill!

We have had so many "girly" chats and there will be many more. I do not need to say much more except that the possibilities ahead of you are limitless. Walk in faith and hope as your name means, Rudaviro, confident in your source. Carry with you gratitude, love, and humility, and let life unfold before you. Mummy prays for you and loves you.

**Runako,**

*"My favourite son"* to which you smile and astutely respond, *"Your only son."* That I have one son is true. That you are my favourite son, as Rudie and Joley are both my favourite daughters, is also just as true.

It has been fourteen years since that first day we met. Wow! I enjoy our time together, as I get to know you a little differently. My little boy has gone and a young man is emerging.

So far, I love this young gentleman before me, who is displaying some very admirable qualities beyond his age. Your passion, discipline, and dedication are next to none and evident on any pitch you play. Always on time, attentive, and respectful towards your family, teachers, coaches, teammates, and numerous friends. Keep doing whatever it is you are doing, and more. We are cheering you on!

You are a star, Atk, the best and most perfect son and brother ever! Your heart is as beautiful as the meaning of your name, Runako-rwashe, a beauty that comes from above and within. No matter what life throws at you, keep that beautiful smile and your brilliance shining. I am excited for your future, my love. Mummy prays for you and loves you.

**Joley,**

*"My cuddles."* Mufaro, joy, and happiness. Carefree, loving, caring, and generous. I love your creativity, your energy, your quick sense of humour, and your sensitivity, too.

My favourite laughs with you so far come with a *Dork Diaries* book last thing at night in a warm, cosy bed. We are due another bookshop visit soon now to make up for time lost during the days of quarantine. Who needs COVID-19 these days, especially when you cannot even cough to clear your throat without being stared at with suspicion!

I wonder what Mackenzie would have to say if anyone dared to cough near her? Let's do the queasy cheesy dance!

Life is beautiful with you in it, Joley Moley. Let us enjoy being ten years old. I look forward to our next city day trip with you. I love you, sweetheart, and I am excited about everything that awaits us on this beautiful mother and daughter journey. Mummy prays for you

# Libby Monica

Libby is an Author. Blogger. Mindset & Empowerment Coach and Mentor.

Her latest publication is an anthology, Letters of Love, written in collaboration with eleven global and best-selling authors. Letters of Love is currently on pre-sale offer with a selection of bonuses.

As well as being an author, Libby has a growth mindset that keeps her open to new experiences, new people, new places, and new things. She invests unapologetically to her own continuous personal and professional development and encourages others to do the same for amazing results and. fulfilling life. Libby supports women to break the chains of anxiety, fear, and a limiting mindset so that they connect with their life purpose and self-worth, becoming confident, vision-driven, and successful.

Her passion is to see people connecting with their north star and living their best life.

email: libby@libbymonica.com

Facebook: https://www.facebook.com/libby.sweetman.9

Website:  www.libbymonica.com

"To the world, you may be one, but to us, you

are our world"

# To My Son, Jasper

Whenever I start writing a letter to you, I have a rush of thoughts enter my mind as to what I want to write, but then it comes time for me to actually put pen to paper and I can never seem to find the right words.

 It is easy with loss to focus on the negative things. It is difficult when faced with such a tragedy to find something positive. That is why this letter to you is different. This letter is going to tell you about the things that losing you has taught me, not only about life in general but also about myself.

*"Grief is a nasty game of feeling the weakest you have ever felt and morphing it into the strongest person you will have to become." - Windgate Lane*

During the first few months following your loss, I constantly thought to myself. I will never have enough strength to get through this, and to be honest I still have days when the rollercoaster of grief starts to sneak up on me and I think that all of my strength has been consumed and wonder how I will manage to find more. It amazes me how much inner strength human beings have, and you have no idea how strong you are until you experience something that requires you to use that strength daily.

I have learnt that inner strength means that you have resilience, perseverance, and tenacity—the power one needs to deal with difficult situations—and these were qualities I never knew I had until I lost you. Every day, I continually question where the extra strength comes from to keep moving forward (I still don't have the answer), but I do constantly remind myself that "the struggle you're in today is developing the strength you need for tomorrow."

*"Grief is like the ocean, it comes in waves ebbing and flowing. Sometimes the water is calm, and sometimes it is overwhelming. All we can do is learn to swim." - Vicki Harrison*

GRIEF ... what a word. The real definition of the word is "intense sorrow, especially caused by someone's death.' I was surprised to find through Google that the word could be summed up in such a short sentence.

I believe that learning the true depth and form of grief in its "purest form" has given me a completely different outlook on life. I have learnt that grief lasts for a lifetime and I will grieve for a lifetime, that there is no "getting over" or "fixing" grief; that for as long as I breathe, I will grieve for you. Grief is a long and tiring journey with many paths, not just one.

Losing you has taught me that grief becomes part of everyday life for a bereaved parent and that it will always be a big part of who I am now. It wasn't really that long after losing you when I realised to survive my future without you, one of the biggest things that I had to do was to accept my grief, welcome my grief (hug my grief), and learn to live with it. By facing it and accepting it, it became easier to live with. To grieve is to love and to love forever is to grieve forever. Grief is the purest form of love, and losing you has shown me just how deep grief and love can go.

*"It has been said, 'time heals all wounds.' I do not agree. The wounds remain. In time, the mind, protecting its sanity, covers them with scar tissue and the pain lessens. But it is never gone." - Rose Kennedy*

I remember hearing from so many people that "time heals all wounds" and that "it will get easier." Losing you has taught me that time does not heal all wounds—whether it was a month after your loss, or a year after your loss (and even just over three years on), the only thing that time does is give me the opportunity to learn how to continue to cope with your loss, and it gives me time to continue to learn how to adapt to my life and future without you. Unfortunately, time is one of my worst enemies because the loss of you feels like only yesterday but also ten years ago at the same time (like being in a crazy time machine).

As each day passes, it means I am one day closer to being able to be with you for eternity; where time will no longer exist, where my pain will no longer exist. Until then, I have found a way to turn the negative aspect of time associated with loss into a positive. I have learnt that time allows me to honour you, to remember you, and to create a legacy for you. Without time, I would not be able to do any of this and more importantly, I have realised that time gives me the opportunity to continue to be your mother.

*"No one else will ever know the strength of my love for you. After all, you are the only one who knows what my heart sounds like from the inside." - Author unknown*

I have learnt, most of the time, people who have never lost a child or baby can't seem to understand (or try to understand) that the love I have for you is ongoing like the love a mother has for a living child. It seems some people think you can suddenly switch the feelings off and that you end up being okay after losing a baby. This is not the case.

Your life and death have taught me that the love and bond between a mother and her child are eternal—it starts through conception and continues to grow and develop throughout pregnancy. Love never dies, so there will never come a time when I will stop loving you. It means that bereaved parents love their children unconditionally, always, and forever, just as parents of living children do.

What society still cannot seem to fully comprehend is that bereaved parents are still parents. I conceived you, I carried you for thirty-seven weeks, and I formed a bond with you that death will never be able to break. No matter what people see or hear me do, I have learnt that most will never be able to comprehend the strength of my love for you.

*"Childloss is never-ending… we are constantly longing for the memories we never created in the future we imagined we would have." - Sandra*

There is so much that losing you has taught me. I have lost other people in my life (even tragically and unexpectedly), but I now know that child loss is never-ending. Your absence is felt daily in all that I do; there are certain times of the year and occasions where your absence is felt more deeply than others, where we should be making new memories together as a family as I had always imagined.

However, this journey taught me that although I may not be able to create the memories with you, I have the opportunity to create memories which include you in them. Just over three years later, I continue to do all that I can to create these new memories and I know I will continue this forever. I choose to try to create something special out of a never-ending roller coaster ride.

*"A meaningful life is not about being rich, being popular, being highly educated or being perfect… it is about being real, being humble, being strong and being able to share ourselves and touch the lives of others." - Author unknown*

When I found out that I was pregnant with you, a lot changed. I changed. Suddenly, my priority in life was to be a better person, to make sure that I would be a mother you could look up to and be proud of. The centre of my universe suddenly shifted and changed, and you became all that mattered, you became more important than life itself. Losing you made me really think about the type of person I wanted to be.

They say when you lose a baby, your whole world changes, and I can honestly say this is true. After spending thirty-seven weeks thinking about the kind of life I wanted to provide for you, the things I wanted us to achieve as a family, and the type of mother I wanted to become (forming my "new normal"), this was suddenly taken away. It felt like I was frozen in time whilst the rest of the world was spinning in fast forward motion all around me. The idea of my future had suddenly come crashing down and when I regained my balance again, I realised that I had to create another "new normal," one that included being a mother to an angel.

Priorities in my life changed, and I had to think about what I wanted to get out of life. This is when I decided that my "new normal" needed to include being humble, being strong, and being able to share my experience with others either by offering guidance and support whenever possible. I continue to do what I can in your memory but to also to share my story in the hopes of being able to help break the silence around baby loss and to try to inspire others, to show them that you can still have a meaningful life when working through the journey of losing a baby.

*"Everyone must leave something behind when they die. Your legacy is every life you touch." - Maya Angelou*

You can't create a legacy to leave behind if you are no longer here to live your life. Losing you taught me that I could create a legacy in your memory. I realised if I wanted you to have a legacy it would be up to me to create one for you and that is what I started to do a few months after you left me. I continually challenge myself to come up with new ideas and ways to add to your legacy and carry it on.

 It started with three fundraisers. On top of this, I joined Still Aware as a volunteer ambassador as well as the International Vasa Previa Foundation, a podcast interview in relation to some of the donations I have made, and the reasoning behind them as well as speaking about my loss to try to help break the silence within society, JJ's Angel Flutters, and of course the opportunity to write this letter as well as other things I am currently working on.

People ask me why I choose to do these things and there is one simple answer: to continue to create a legacy in my son's memory.

Apart from creating a legacy for you, these are all positive things that I can do in such a traumatic and deeply painful time. The death of you doesn't take away or change the fact that I am your mother and always will be, and therefore just as parents to living children do all that they can for them, I will continue to do all that I can for you. This is what you deserve.

*"I forgot to read the fine print when I signed up to be your mum. I thought it would be hugs and smiles and quite a lot of fun. I did not see the bit that read of pain, loss, grief, and despair. I did not know that you would be gone, and that life would be unfair. But I am still your mother, I will be every day. If I had to read the fine print, I would have signed up anyway." - Karen Prisca*

Being your mother is still the best gift I could have been given and nothing, not even death, can ever take that motherhood away from me. Losing you has taught me so much—about life and about myself, it has (and continues) to challenge me every day, in both positive and negative ways. I learn to survive your leaving as each new day comes because each day you are still gone. Some things don't get better, but somehow I continue to get stronger, I continue to learn to live with my situation, I fix what I can and adapt to what I can't and ensure that I take nothing for granted.

 I will never be fully okay, but I'm here, I'm still trying, I'm doing the best I can (as ugly and messy as that may be), and I continue to challenge myself to be the best version of myself that I can possibly be, in your memory, in the hopes that you would be looking down on me and proud to call me your mum—and that is worth celebrating (I think anyway).

I am and always will be proud to call you my son. I just wish that you were in my arms instead of in my heart, but I thank you for choosing me to be your mother and allowing me to learn these things about life and about myself. I will continue to be your legacy, I will continue to be your voice, and every morning I wake up to face a new day, I choose to honour you by living my life.

May we meet again.

Love always from your mum.

xxx

# Sarah Pridham

I never would have expected to be twenty-seven years old and experiencing one of the hardest journeys that life can throw at you.

After being born and raised in Adelaide, South Australia as an only child, I moved to a small town on the Yorke Peninsula to start my life with my partner. We have been together for nearly now been married for six years and have one child, our angel son, Jasper.

Apart from working full time in Administration and Sales, I use my spare time doing all that I can to continue Jasper's memory and legacy. I also try to provide as much support and guidance to other bereaved parents during their journey of loss as I can.

To you, dearest in my heart,

# My Love Anchor:
# A Letter of Legacy

You stand behind me, cheering me forward.

The vision of you has encouraged me to unlock my words and life wisdom. To be myself with you.

Life can be messy. You know this. You dream, you hope, you expect. You've experienced the crushing, and it leads you to fall apart or it puts a serious chink in your day.

You need a love anchor in times like these. A trustworthy foundation to return to when life becomes overwhelming and crippling.

The ultimate expression of love, this anchor, is the TRUTH. It carries me through every trial and tribulation. Every inevitability of a fallen, sinful world. I found HOPE through the truth and want to share it with you...

There are four types of love from the Greek:

*Eros* - Romantic love

*Phileo or Philia* - Brotherly/friendship love

*Storge* - Empathetic love

*Agape* - God's unconditional love for us

**Eros- Romantic Love:**

I found love in marriage. But not the way that I expected.

It took years for me to shake the societal definition of what love is. The fairytale story, the locking of eyes in that perfect moment. The emotional rush of natural chemistry and everything falling into place because love fixes everything. If we just had that spouse, that partner, that soulmate doing what we want and pleasing us because we deserve it, we'd be happy.

That's what we are told, right?

**The Reality**

That's not how things have worked in my life or in the many lives of those I have counseled. What I learned about love defies every societal norm and belief.

> *"Love isn't about you.*
>
> *Love is about the other person.*
>
> *Whether in marriage, friendship, family,*
>
> *or reaching out to the broken, hurting, and less fortunate."*

If you dig deeper at the root of our society's definition of love, you'll find a two-letter word: "ME."

How can I please myself? How can I make myself happy? How can I fulfil MY heart's desires?

We try to say it's about others. But is it?

The secret to love in my marriage that stands the test of time is found in this book in my letter to my husband.

**Philia- Friendship/Brotherly/Family Love:**

Love is self-sacrificial. Some days I'm exhausted, dealing with my own life crises. You contact me needing desperate help, advice, or to process. I do my best to fit you in my full schedule because you matter. You're on my mind constantly.

"Giving of yourself is tiring, but rewarding. Love others like I am loving you. It will bless you and them."

My dearest friends/family, I can't say enough how much I love you and see you as a blessing. I appreciate the creative ways we've met each other's needs. You've encouraged me to process my thoughts and emotions. You have told me to never give up, to live transparently, and speak the unpopular truth.

I am honored and privileged to serve you in my ministry, *"Scripture Prescriptions."*

You've touched hearts. You're making a difference in a beautiful domino effect, using, practicing, and sharing the tools I've given you with others. You influence and touch mine, which pours out into your spheres. Did you know that?

Don't ever stop being who you are and giving of yourself. Your effect is concentric and expands beyond who you know.

**Storge- Empathetic Love:**

Love is an action. Not an emotion. We get this wrong all the time. Love is a choice we make. It rejects pride, arrogance, rudeness, irritability, impatience, and more.

You never know what someone is going through, their perspective on life and their past. Don't respond to the unkind and harsh with hostility. Hard shells can be softened and broken, but it takes time. LISTEN. If they are willing, they could be your next breakthrough.

The type of empathy that lifts people out of depression, mental health challenges, and cycles of despair is in this scenario:

*You sit in a muddy puddle, soaked and cold. This is THE WORST day. You cry so much from frustration, despair, anger, and every emotion that exists; your tears mix with the water and run out.*

I see you. I do not sit with you like you're used to. I stand on the edge with a freshly heated towel, reach out my hand to yours and lift. I wrap you up and we walk together to heal with the truth and tools to manage life. The misery becomes your distant memory and testimony.

This is the type of empathy that leads to victory in one's life. If you can find that in your heart, you will change lives one measured, empathetic action at a time.

The love examples above sound hopeful, positive, and uplifting. I've devoted myself to living them as a lifestyle, but they are impossible to accomplish on your own. You need *"agape."*

**Agape- God's unconditional love for us**

Agape love is defined in secular society as the love for humanity or charity toward humanity. But it comes from the Greek, which means a higher level of unconditional love from God toward each other.

We need this love poured into us to pour out into others. It's not of our own power, but that of a higher power. God IS love. (1 John 4:7-12)

The ultimate gift and demonstration of love is the sacrifice of a sinless, perfect Jesus Christ dying for OUR sins and resurrecting from the dead so we can have eternal life with Him forever. What love is greater than choosing undeserved death for an undeserved us?

I received this gift of Jesus Christ's salvation into my heart for the forgiveness of my sins long ago. From a deep, intimate relationship with Him, I've been able to love all those around me with that unconditional love that God has for me. That is the only way we can truly love the way we desire to love.

*"We love because He first loved us." - 1 John 4:19*

That is how I LOVE YOU.

All my love,

Rebekah J. Samuel

My darling Jason,

# You and I: A Love Letter From A Neurodiverse to Her Neurotypical

Because of my autism, expression of emotions can be difficult, but I want to give you something to cherish forever. I pray this Valentine's Day gift touches your heart and speaks to you how I feel when writing it. I hope this letter lives beyond our existence, is a source of healing in marriages, and preparation for those who desire it.

*You and I are building our marriage castle. Every year a new set of bricks are forged from mixing and molding. We lay them in the foundation with every intentional act of trust in faith.*

Saying those vows, little did you and I know how much would be navigated in six short years. Loss of a car, two diagnoses: One PTSD and the other autism. Multiple anxiety attacks. Heaps of apologies, loads of forgiveness. Two military moves from coast to coast. Four moves in five years. The loss of two beloved ones. Working in shared space, in our respective gifts during a pandemic.

From the moment you and I met, I knew you were different. You are my challenge and my joy. I needed

it. I just didn't know how.

Remember "Oceans?"

"Spirit lead me where my trust is without borders."

Marriage to you was the biggest leap of trust and faith. That lyric was my heart's prayer as I walked down the aisle to the unknown. The best choice of my life.

*Inside this castle, we minister to each other and those outside. Taking care of the ones in need, returning to one another for refreshment and recharging. You and I are dedicated to our callings. Respect for each other is in this castle. They cannot exist apart.*

You know I'm not a gushy, affectionate romantic. You and I were given nerdy, intellectual brains. Add my brain processing difference I'm learning about this year, and some may think us a boring married couple with no spice or life. Yet, our love is unique and inspiring. It means more than recycled love words and phrases.

Our marriage stands out. Not just to you and I, darling, but those who watch. Lots of eyes are on us. What I hope they see the most, my love, is God has loved you and me more than we deserve. He has kept us, guided us, shined the light in the dark areas, and illuminated our paths.

I love that we have a passion for ministry, through different avenues, divine and perfectly designed.

I have deep empathy, and you help me navigate that

in a healthy way with others. I'm sorry when I don't always listen. When I want my own way. Apologies and forgiveness are a beautiful and necessary part of our marriage.

You were never the initial dream, but are the dream I truly wanted. I had no idea what was possible or capable. Heck, I didn't even know myself until this year. You've introduced me to a whole new world. It shattered my expectations of what life can be, even with life's mental health challenges.

You and I are opposites in most of our interests, but what society tells us about this is just lies. Loyalty and self-sacrifice have consistently helped us share ourselves. You make me laugh and I genuinely enjoy our time spent together. All those memes. :D

You accept me. You tell me to be myself and not be someone I'm not. To avoid masking. Selfless and kind love.

You know the times when I go mute, when words are non-existent, and it's not because I'm being manipulative or giving you the silent treatment. You're patient, love.

I am overwhelmed at times when I am thinking about you. How much of a blessing you've been to my life and how much I appreciate all of you. Your steadiness is tenacious. Your generous heart is infectious. There's just so much about you, Jason, that can't fit in one letter. I am so grateful that we have till death do us part to express it all.

*Inside this castle, we have damage, and patching that is needed. You and I do not abandon the unfinished work. We courageously enter the darkest, scariest, less traveled hallways. You and I.*

You and I don't have the cookie-cutter Hallmark love story. We faced trials even before we sealed our love before God. That didn't stop us. You and I handled those trials and continue to, pushing through them. Psh! You and I are too competitive to give up. ;)

You're my pillar. God established this and confirmed it. You hold me, you support me, and you keep me grounded. When I learned about my autism, it felt like my world was crumbling to pieces. I thought you'd leave me like so many others do. It can be a burdensome task. A wife with PTSD and autism.

I am grateful it's YOU who He picked.

You foresee my meltdowns and snuggle me. You encourage my stims. You are steadfast. Immovable. It makes me cry thinking about it. How someone can be so loved. But that's YOU. You love me; all of me. Even more, your devotion to God and His Word is dedicated. That makes me love you more.

Our marriage is a testimony of God placed in the center. It reflects a committed union, a love beyond the romantic, emotional centered love we recognize. A love rooted and anchored to last. It's not a love for ourselves. It's a love that is infused with the unconditional love of God, the greatest love of all.

*This castle holds a legacy. It has purposes, displaying God's glory. Though it sometimes feels like YOU AND I because of our vast differences in mind, emotions, and being…*

Truly, it's always been about WE.

WE have found our romance; WE have found our love; WE have found our joy and happiness. WE do not expect it to just exist. WE have built it.

WE will always win.

I LOVE YOU, JASON.

Forever and always yours,

Rebekah

# Rebekah J. Samuel

Rebekah, aka The Lady Gadget, is a late-identified Autistic, small business owner, ministry/community coordinator, and military spouse.

Her natural knack for problem-solving, networking, tech support, building systems, and vocal/instrumental skills help her serve actively in her churches and communities, as she and her husband travel coast to coast in the constantly moving military lifestyle.

Rebekah passionately works with her fellow neuro-diverse and neuro-typical individuals around the globe toward the healing of unresolved church/faith/spiritual abuse, trauma, broken relationships, and mental health challenges. She loves to impact lives through her words and voice on social media, YouTube, podcasts, and radio.

In her tech business, The Lady Gadget, she provides affordable custom branded website/blog services and offers tech troubleshooting support.

Rebekah is a dedicated wife, community coordinator, helper, mentor, teacher, author, and friend.

To connect with Rebekah, you can find her here:

https://www.rebekahjsamuel.com

# Double The Love, A Letter To My Twins

To my husband, Arthur Darivas,

who has shared the journey with me

## One and Two

My husband and I are in hospital. I am having a check-up as something is not quite right. We spend hours in the waiting room; it's full. I know I am pregnant, and for a while, I can't help to think that I am having a miscarriage.

The nurse calls my name. We enter the small cubicle where they take tests and check my health, and the doctor comes and says, "Well, you are going to get an ultrasound."

We wait even more until the nurse comes and takes us to the ultrasound room. The screen is on, my belly is prepared, and the doctor starts the procedure. He points to a small dot inside me. "Here is the baby," he says.

I smile, and he continues scrutinizing my belly, looking at the screen. Another dot appears. "There are two here!" he says. "You are expecting two babies.

I am so happy to still be pregnant that I don't quite process the big news. My husband is in a bit of a shock and in a way, I am too because all I can think is, *Good, the baby is still here.* Well, this explains you being unwell," he points out, "so go home and rest."

It took me a few days to really understand that I was having two babies at the same time. I remember calling my parents; they were very happy. My dad was a bit worried for me, for the responsibility that means to be a parent of multiples.

We were living in Denver, Colorado at that time. However, the universe had other plans for your arrival in this world, my kids.

During my pregnancy, my husband was busy working and got offered an opportunity to come back to Australia in a new position. It was in Sydney where the first two-and-a-half years of your life took place. After that, we went to live in Chile, my birth country, and then back again to Australia. We are a kind of gypsy family.

However, I do not want to enter into an account of our life together. My intention with this letter of love is to address each of you individually first, and then touch base on a few things I want you to keep in your minds and hearts for years to come.

I will start with the eldest of you by three minutes...

## Marcus

I remember you at about ten months old, in hospital, with nurses getting you ready for surgery. I stood by your side and I sang to you "*arrurrú* my baby, *arrurrú* my son, *arrurú* piece of my heart" (a closer translation from Spanish) while nurses placed all the needles in your little arms. You looked at me in awe and I knew you were listening to me; you did not cry and I saw love in your eyes because I was looking at you in the same way.

That was one of the times I remember feeling the invisible power of Love doing its magic.

You have always been a loving soul. You hug people in a way that makes them feel welcomed and acknowledged, and you show your love in the little details. For example, I recall a time when we were on holidays in beautiful north Chile, and we were walking through the handcraft market and you picked a little stuffed llama for my father, your grandfather, so he would remember us when looking at it.

We were living in Australia at the time.

How many times have we been walking on the streets and I heard your voice say, "Mum, do you have a coin?" because you cannot bear to see a homeless person asking for money without feeling their trouble in your heart. You are compassionate and caring.

Perhaps the most striking attribute you have is your loyalty and love for your friends. Do you remember your joy when playing with them, how proud you were showing them your toys and sharing with them? Your first friend was Shusaku, a nice boy from Japan. Your friendship was so strong that it is still in your heart and I know that we owe you a trip to Japan. That trip will happen one day.

Friendship is a high-frequency word for you. You treasure the moments spent with friends in Chile, Melbourne, and Sydney, and I know that more friends are coming your way here in the UK, our home now. Those that will appreciate your sharp sense of humour, your love of football, music, and movies will see that you are a very good bloke with a big heart.

Marcus, *te amo!*

# Olivia

I remember you at eighteen months old, trying to stop me when I was moving Marcus's cradle to another room because the two of you were waking each other up at night. It was time for you to be in separate rooms.

You were in front of me, putting your little arms up and saying, "No, no, Ma, Ma," referring to your brother. I knew it was hard for you, however, it was even harder to see you both trying to sleep and being cranky the next day. I always wondered what you were thinking.

From the very beginning, you showed a warrior spirit. Determination has been the quality imprinted in your heart, the one quality that has been pivotal in your journey to be the young intelligent, and caring woman you are becoming now. We share a common interest in matters of the soul, we both love art, philosophy, and fashion although I know you would like me to dress in a more trendy way.

My mind goes back to Stockholm, Sweden where you and I lived for six months. You were healing from a difficult illness that required us to leave Australia for a while. It was there where we cemented a strong mother and daughter relationship because we beat the illness together, trusting our divine guides, practicing the teachings of the Cyclopea Method, knitting, painting, crafting, and later visiting that amazing city. We promised to go back, to say thank you and to visit once more the beautiful old town, this time with the eyes of health and love.

Your love for learning different languages has made you a worldly young lady and I know that France is awaiting you with open arms, now more mature, more knowledgeable, more *you*. Your abilities in art are outstanding and I always enjoy seeing you producing a masterpiece. I am sure that one day your drawings and paintings will be on exhibition in important art galleries and you will leave your blueprint in the world.

Olivia, *te amo!*

## Twins

You are both very different, not only because you are a boy and a girl, but because you have your own individual ways of being and seeing the world. However, there is always an invisible cord between you, a cord that unites you beyond time and space. I have photos of you sleeping in your baby rocking chairs exactly in the same position, one arm up, the other one down, head slightly turned to the same side.

I particularly remember a day when Olivia was in France on an exchange program and Marcus was in Sydney. Olivia called me crying because of a small problem and just with an hour difference, Marcus arrived from school crying, too. In a few minutes, everything was solved, but I was a bit taken back by the invisible energy linking you far across the world.

I always remind you that one day your dad and I will not be here to hold you and even if you have your own family by then, you have each other. You are tied in the unseen power of love.

# The year of resilience

We all know that year 2020 was particularly hard for humanity, for planet Earth. The world continues changing and it is going to take some time to see how much we have transformed as human beings, both collectively and individually. Across the planet, people have been finding roads to mend, to improve, to innovate, to reinvent themselves and I firmly believe that for every bad situation lived something good comes out the other side.

We, as a family, lived both wonderful moments of joy and moments of tremendous pain. We got away with several learnings about our own capacity to rise, to elevate ourselves from any hard scenario we might be living. Resilience is a quality that most of us have and is directly powered by love because we find strength inside our hearts, minds, and bodies and the little love we might feel goes toward our well-being.

I am writing about resilience particularly because I want to say that I am extremely proud of you, Marcus and Olivia, for the way you take this word into action. I am sure that all the events experienced during 2020 have ingrained in you both the qualities of forgiveness, kindness, and gratitude.

Now happiness is around the corner, make sure to see it in what really matters.

## Love

My dear kids, I want to talk a little bit about love, about the concept of love I would like to pass on to you.

For me, love is not just "human" love, is not the love of attachments, is not the love of jealousy or possessions. Love is an invisible force uniting absolutely everything in the universe. I first heard about this notion of love from Fresia Castro, my spiritual mentor, creator of the Cyclopea Method, and it made total sense to me, but furthermore, I have experienced real love in me.

Love is fluid, it is energy coming from the Source, God, Spirit, and it runs through all of us. We are able to be here in this world because of love and that common thread shared by everyone makes us equal in all aspects. Love comes from the Source, enters us, fills us, and then we expand it. Only when we feel loved by that superior origin  we are loving ourselves, and this in turn makes us love others.

You see, love acts in a three-way current that allows us to love ourselves, our partners, our family members, our friends, our pets, and everything else because it comes from the Source and is the Source at the same time. Love is circular; its life, its creation.

I have been teaching this concept of love to other people for years now, and it is the only intangible thing I can leave as a legacy for you both. Go to the world, always connected to the Source, the way I have shown you. Inhale love, expand love, be radiant beings, change the world.

# Mum's Time

*To Marcus and Olivia*

A poem from my heart

I carried you
I washed you
I dressed you
I fed you
I chauffeured you
I LOVE you
I guided you
I supported you
I understood you
I admired you
I got you
I LOVE you
I feel you
I encourage you
I cheer for you
I shield you
I help you
I LOVE you
I kiss you
I hug you
I listen to you
I counsel you
I smile at you
I LOVE you
I AM always here for you

I LOVE you!

*"Wherever you are, and whatever you do, be in love." Rumi*

# Veronica Sanchez

Veronica is originally from Santiago, Chile and also an Australian citizen. She has been writing for many years for online magazines and blogs in Spanish and English. Veronica is a Number 1 bestselling author with her book *Positive Habits, 21 Words That Transform Your Life Daily*.

Veronica is a teacher of grammar and literature in Spanish. During the last ten years, she has dedicated herself to spirituality and is a Spiritual Awakening Teacher. She is a Certified Instructor for the Cyclopea Method of Internal Activation of the Pineal Gland (Third Eye), a method created thirty years ago in South America by the Latin spiritual leader Fresia Castro. Veronica, so far, is the only instructor in the world teaching this life-changing method in English.

Apart from teaching and writing, Veronica loves reading, travelling, and spending time with family and friends.

Veronica and her family moved to the UK at the beginning of 2020 and they are waiting for the world to open up and start exploring beautiful Europe.

Facebook: https://www.facebook.com/veroteacher

Instagram: http://www.instragram.com/veronicasmentor

LinkedIn: http://www.linkedin.com/in/veronicasanchezmentor

Website: http://www.highfrequencybeing.com

# Dear Wonderful Self

You have been on my mind a lot lately. There is so much I want to say to you and that I hope you really hear and believe with all your being. Yet, for reasons which I am now coming to understand in a fuller way, there are lots of feelings that I have not expressed to you.

We have been together for a very long time; our whole life, as a matter of fact. And I know for a fact that sadly, I have not always shown you and given you the love you absolutely deserve. So part of my reason for writing this letter to you is to make a commitment to being more loving with you each and every day for the rest of my life. I also wish to show you how much you are loved not only by me!

Recently, I read a passage about relationships. It talked about the variety of relationships we have in a lifetime, from the relationships with our parents, siblings, friends, colleagues, and lovers. It concluded by saying that the longest relationship we will ever have is the relationship with ourselves. At the time, I remember thinking how true and powerful that statement was. We can't run away from ourselves. So rather than hating on ourselves, why not consider loving ourselves instead?

As with anything in life, it is a journey and a continual practice. It's not like you wake up and automatically love yourself. It is a daily commitment and action to love yourself. This letter is one step in showing you how much I love you.

Each and every day for the rest of my life, I vow to take small actions to show you how much I love you. And whilst I do not have rose-coloured glasses on, I do know that there will be days I will struggle to be loving towards you. However, I will do my best to find even the smallest thing to love about you on those days.

For many years, it looks like you had a heavy curtain over your eyes, shrouding your life in a certain level of darkness. Over the course of the last few years, it seems that the curtain is slowly rising. I see you embodying a kinder and more loving attitude towards yourself. My wish for you is to feel the love others feel for you and give yourself that love.

I am seeing that, in the past, I treated you terribly. I was extremely good at criticizing you and running you down. The venom that has sometimes spewed from my mouth towards you was unquestionably and completely unnecessary and uncalled for. What was the benefit of me saying all those things? There was no benefit to hurting you with the words I thought and said.

Yes, there have been people around you that encouraged and cultivated an atmosphere of self-hatred and loathing. I am delighted to see that you have learnt that those who demonstrate such outward hatred towards others also do that to themselves. This is not your burden to wear. This is not your responsibility. And most happily, I notice those people are no longer part of your life. In this action alone, you demonstrate a much healthier love for yourself.

I feel like an apology is really the elephant in the

room. I am sorry that I did not show you the full depths of my affection, my love, and my respect. You deserve infinitely more love than I have previously demonstrated and given.

And let me say that you are the most precious of all beings I have ever had the good fortune to meet. As Shakespeare said, let me count the ways I love you...

You have had many hurdles to overcome, so much loss and grief to contend with. I love the way you reframed the heartbreaking loss of many pregnancies into a vision of those cherished bebes dancing around you, always with you, with their angel wings. I love that you have come to terms with such devastating grief.

You face and overcome daily challenges that even have the experts around you, shaking their heads in disbelief thinking, "How does she do it?" Yet, each day, you get up, put a smile on your face, and find the courage to face the day ahead.

One of the things I admire most about you is your ability to keep on going even when things are difficult; even when you feel you do not have the strength to go on, somehow you do. Each and every day, you keep on going. That, my darling, is phenomenal resilience.

Your courage and bravery is another quality I truly and deeply admire about you. The last few years have forced you to continually dig into a well of courage that no one could have foreseen you would need or that indeed you had. You have made decisions that were absolutely the right and best for you and your children, yet truthfully terrified the living daylights out of you.

You have faced death head-on. The way you continue to hold yourself in the face of such adversity is inspiring. The grace you exude is breath-taking.

Love is a topic you spend a lot of time exploring and contemplating. One could say that you love love! I know for a fact that one of your favourite lines is from *Moulin Rouge*: "The greatest thing you'll ever learn is just to love and be loved in return." And in essence, I think that is the meaning you want to put into your life.

Love is what makes our lives worth living, it can bring us the greatest frustrations and the greatest joys. Loving you is a privilege and an honour.

I know you have not been overly fortunate in matters of the heart. You have loved deeply, yet you question whether that love was reciprocated. I know I can't speak conclusively or decisively for others, however, I can say that you are well-loved by those who know you. Often they have ways of expressing their love, which leaves you questioning whether you are indeed loved and lovable. Please know that you are loved so deeply.

Over the years, you have had a few people tell you wonderful things about yourself. I have seen it and heard it. For reasons I don't understand, you did not take their words with the intention they were said or given. One of my wishes for you is for you to hear and feel all the love that others have given you and will give you in the years to come.

In year nine, your favourite teacher, Mr Harris, dropped a bombshell in English class one day. The class was talking about relationships, and I think it might have been in relation to *Romeo and Juliet*. Mr Harris said that if you can't or don't love yourself, no one else will love you either. It was probably one of the most valuable lessons in those high school years.

What you struggled to do and apply to yourself was how to actually love yourself. You can see the beauty in others so readily, yet giving yourself that tenderness, that love, that kindness, and compassion has been incredibly difficult for you.

That is the thing I would like to change the most. I want you to feel like you are loved.

I know over the years you have found it difficult to reconcile loving yourself and being concerned with the perceptions of others. I know you grew up in a culture where being seen to love yourself was considered pompous and arrogant. Thankfully, this is less the case now as we talk more and more about self-love. There is greater recognition that loving yourself is actually really important for your well-being.

Over the years, I have learnt a lot about what you love and what you don't like so much. I have learnt what brings you joy and heartache. I have seen you struggle and rise like the phoenix. I have seen you forge a path where there was none.

You have put in the effort to find your way. I have seen you stand with poise and elegance, then unexpectedly and magnificently reveal yourself. You have the ability to captivate people and leave them sighing in delight, much like a peacock revealing his wondrous feathers.

You have a beauty that is mesmerizing, both internal and external. You have a heart that is truly golden and wishes well for everyone, no matter the situation. Your desire, willingness, and capacity to forgive others despite the great hurt they have inflicted on you is inspirational. You lead the way in matters of the heart.

Please learn to turn that love inwards as well. You need to give that love freely and readily to yourself in much the same way that you give it to others. You are worthy and deserving of that love.

Take a moment to imagine how luscious and sensational it would feel to be truly loved.

Think about how it would feel in your body. How would your body feel if it felt truly, deeply loved? I know you keep seeing all the flaws because others have pointed things out or made cruel comments. You do not need to take those opinions on. Do they matter anymore?

Choose love and kindness to your body. Cherish how marvelously it enables you to do all the amazing things you do every day.

Now think about how it would be to offer yourself words of encouragement, appreciation, and validation instead of criticism and pointing out all the things you think you do wrong. Believe me, very few around you will say you are failing or doing wrong. You have the ability to provide that love to yourself. You can love yourself in exactly the ways you know and need to be loved. And with that, know how much I also love and cherish you.

My deepest wish for you is for you to know that you are indeed lovable and worthy. You are one of the most amazing people I have ever met, and I say that without being conceited or sarcastic.

You are a strong, resilient, courageous, creative, inspiring, and inspired woman. You deserve all the love you give to others to be turned inwards to yourself regularly.

You are loved so very much.

All my love,

Kerri-Ann

Love moves like the wind

Sometimes a gentle breeze

Sometimes it moves everything in its path

Love is our greatest unseen dance

In a daily tango with the sun and moon

Love is the tie that binds us

Love is the most beautiful word

- Kerri-Ann Sheppard

# Kerri-Ann Sheppard

Kerri-Ann has been writing for almost as long as she can talk! When she picked up her first pencil, she started scribbling and the writing has not yet stopped. Her friends and family say that "words are her thing."

She has a passion for words, writing, and reading. Over the years, writing has been a constant companion. She writes when faced with the darkest of times and in the most wondrous of times. Kerri-Ann is keen to share how writing has helped her and can help others and their well-being.

Kerri-Ann is a solo mama-bear to two amazing special needs children who consume almost every moment of the day. When there is a quiet moment, Kerri-Ann loves to write. Other sanity savers for Kerri-Ann include a near-constant stream of mildly warm tea, chocolate that she begrudgingly shares, kitty cat cuddles, and boxing sessions at the gym (who knew boxing could be so therapeutic!).

Letters of Love is the first anthology for Kerri-Ann in 2021.

Kerri-Ann can be found at kaswrites.com

I dedicate this Love Letter to myself, my Higher-Self, and all Lost Souls out in the abyss. You're not alone and you're loved

# Star-Crossed Lovers

Shh ... someone's coming. I must be quiet. I must be still.

I could hear the leaves crunch below my feet with every step I took through the Forest of Sorrows. I never thought I would reach this place. There was a sense of familiarity as if somewhere in a distant memory I had been here before.

One foot in front of the other, step by step. That's how this journey began.

The lantern flickered as a gust of wind picked up, illuminating my face and then something else just off in the distance. A few of her leaves danced their way down to the forest floor. It was as if they shimmered in the reflection of the lantern and the stars above.

This is what I was looking for ... You.

The Tree Woman.

There she was in her magnificence, illuminated by her inner brilliance, but hiding away in the dense fog of separation and masked with a scarlet blindfold. My heart ached for her, how alone she must feel out here in these woods. Yet ... at the same time, I felt such unconditional love for what she was, is, and will become.

I smiled as I walked over. Had I been walking for days? Or maybe it was months, or was it years? Time felt unreal at this moment, a combination of all my life events that led up to this very singular point in time.

It was as if this moment had been calling to me all of my life, beckoning me to begin this journey. Just so I could find you. So that we could connect. Working our way to each other, me backward and you forwards.

I pinched myself to make sure this was real. My skin on my wrist turned pink as a tingle went through my arm. Yes, this was in fact real.

I knew I had to be slow and delicate. Much like approaching a deer in the wilderness, again one step at a time.

I approached her, and my fingertips touched her trunk; she shuddered, almost pulling herself backward. I quickly pulled my hand away.

 Don't worry, I'm not here to hurt you. I've been looking for you for what feels like an entire lifetime. Please, reveal yourself. It was destined that I come here and find you. For you and I are one, we are the same, I ... you, and you ... I.

That's when the tree began to move. Out of the bark, she appeared more clearly.  I paused again for a sliver of a moment in pure awe.

Her weeping willow leaves transformed into long

locks of hair. She was half tree and half woman. She asked, How are you me, and I you? That seems impossible.

I reached up to the scarlet blindfold she had on. If you just allow me to remove this, I can show you. As I touched the blindfold with my fingers to pull it down, she shifted back into a tree, echoing, I'm not ready.

I whispered, You don't have to hide anymore. For you are safe and won't ever be alone again. In fact, you've never been alone. I know you sense something familiar. The energy we are exchanging. Can you sense it? Can't you feel your roots interconnected?

She began slowly reappearing before my eyes. I don't feel connected; I don't even feel my roots any more. I believe I have heard your voice before, in my darkest of moments, darker than what I can't see now. How can that be?

I sat and leaned my head against her trunk, her legs forming just above the roots, her weeping willow hair dangling over me. I played with it affectionately and gently.

You've heard me before because time and space are limitless and intertwined. The past, the now, and the future are all moments working together across the planes of existence. We have been making our way to each other for the entirety of our lives.

You and me, lovely, we're Star-Crossed Lovers. Can't you feel it in your heart? Can't you feel it in my touch? Just let me show you.

I heard her take a deep breath and let out a long, emotional sigh. But where I am is comfortable. I just have to stay still and quiet. I am safe here ... well, as safe as I will ever be.

The fire from the lantern warmed her branch-like arms. My hands traced the length of them. I walked around her, taking her powerful form in.

Sure, you could stay here, peacefully ignorant to the beauty and opportunity that awaits you. To the internal happiness you can gain from being brave. But now that I have told you ... haven't you felt something awaken?

Her hands dropped down, tracing my face. Feeling the shape and warmth. Are you sure you're not tricking me?

No. I'm the one person who'd never trick you. As I said, I have been here all along. Perhaps not physically, but always there in the back of your mind. You've become strong enough to bring me into your reality. I am only here because you beckoned me, because a part of you is ready. I am your Truthteller.

Her breath quivered, Okay. I am afraid, but now I am curious and would like to see the reality before me, the possibilities ahead.

Making my way to the front of her, I gently took hold of the scarlet blindfold, releasing it and watching it fall to the ground. She gasped as she looked right at my face.

You are my reflection, and I am yours. Infinitely.

She began to radiant, an inner brilliance was finally emerging. Flowers began to sprout from her leaves. Her aura began to shift through colours, as if a prism was surrounding her. Her prism shield. This was just the beginning.

Then her gaze began to shift past me and around her. The fog began to drift away, and she began to weep.

There were millions of others, just like her here. All lost in the Forest of Sorrows, lost in their sadness, all wearing blindfolds, all afraid to make a sound, to move, to feel, or breathe. They were locked in their tree forms, waiting to wake up. They were all just like her, scared and feeling totally alone. Except they weren't alone. They never were. Just like she wasn't alone anymore. She never was. She only thought she was.

The Tree Woman looked around. But what about the others?

I wrapped my arms around her, Don't worry ... one by one, we will help each other escape this place. We will connect with each of their Higher-Selves. They've been whispering to them for some time now, but we will help them find their beating hearts, their will, and their inner love. Their Higher-Self will emerge if you're brave enough to leave. We have much to do.

I reached out my hand.

It's time that we meld into each other. It's time to start our life with true purpose and unconditional love. Now is the time, and the time is now. I am here to guide you out of this place, for I love you. Always have and always will.

With that small gesture of trust and love, we began to fade into each other, transforming into our purest form.

Her roots disintegrated into the forest floor. I saw them move through the dirt, going to other trees. As they did, those Souls began to awaken. The process had started, for when we heal ourselves, it spreads to the souls around us and they unknowingly can begin to awaken.

One foot in front of the other, we began leaving the Forest of Sorrows. Holding the lantern, we looked back one last time. Knowing that we would see all of these Souls again, for we were interconnected, intertwined in time.

You're not alone, you never were, and always remember I love you.

# Abigail Sinclaire

Abigail Sinclaire created Become Bright Within Coaching where she helps survivors of dysfunctional families learn to heal their inner child, ancestral wounds, and connect to their Higher-Self in order to live abundantly and to be who they were meant to be in this lifetime.

Abigail is also the founder and CEO of Human Network Connection where she helps entrepreneurs and virtual media hosts connect, share, and grow with a PR and Media Directory with over 350 connections. She's also the creator of Inspired Connections Vlogazine and is always looking for contributors for articles and videos.

Website - https://www.humannetworkconnection.com

A Love of Letter: My Letter of Love to my beloved mom who left us forever due to complications from a stroke

# Stroke Strike, Three Times

*I am a fighter. Nothing in life is permanent as long as I*

*decide today and never look back. I can rise from anything,*

*especially from my stroke, with God's help.*

The year was 2015, a fantastic year for my business. The team started with just two of us and increased to six. But then, December came, and from then on, not only my life but also my family and my business changed.

That was when I suffered my first Ischemic stroke. Just as I was still coming to terms with the situation, I suffered my second stroke just two weeks later. The two strokes also caused the retina on my right eye to detach. From that point on, one side of my vision was complete darkness while the other was just a blur.

A few months later, while I was trying to cope with the situation, I suffered yet another stroke and my life was never the same again.

I became an infant. I had to learn how to talk because my speech was slurred. I had to learn how to eat—how to chew and swallow—so that whatever I consumed did not end up choking me instead. I had to learn how to climb stairs, how to hold a pen, pick up coins, how to tie my shoelaces, how to button my shirt, and many other simple daily tasks.

But that was nothing compared to how the strokes affected the rest of my life. It affected my energy levels, my ability to walk, my attention level, my memory, my mobility; everything.

The multiple strokes hindered the doctors' attempts to reattach my retina. I had to learn to live in darkness. When they finally managed to operate on my eye, however, life decided that it was not done with me. That same retina detached again after a few weeks and I had to go through a series of eye surgeries just to get my vision back.

The physical therapy from the stroke was exhausting. I had to be confined to a bed and restricted indoors even after I was discharged from the hospital. I did not have the strength to move around on my own, even if I used a walking stick. Someone had to accompany me everywhere I went. I lost count of the number of times I visited the hospital in those four years. It became a second home.

I was sad and my self-esteem suffered because I was a totally different person from who I was prior to the stroke. I used to be cheerful and outgoing. The nature of my business required me to always be surrounded and engaging with people. Suddenly, because of the stroke, I became a hermit and was isolated from the world.

We Need Your Motivation & Inspiration

The journey to recovery is a long and tiring process. It took me three years before I was able to walk on my own without a walking stick. After countless times practicing on my speech, I was finally able to talk without slurring. I started to be able to do things independently. During those days, I got connected with other stroke patients and survivors.

This is my appeal to the world...

As stroke patients and survivors, we need a lot of motivation and inspiration from you, but in a positive way. We do not need your pity or your apologies. I know you mean well, but those words can actually make us feel even worse.

What we need is to connect with the world, to "borrow" its strengths to help us lift our spirits. The change in our physical appearance will likely push us into isolation, so we need your assurance that we are not alone.

Suffering a stroke may affect us physically and emotionally, but not intellectually. Please do not perceive us as victims but as survivors. We need your help to get us to focus on our recovery. Help guide us towards recovery, and not let us dwell on what happened or why.

Not every stroke symptom is immediately visible, but they are very real. Can you imagine living a life that changes 360-degrees within the blink of an eye? You are suddenly faced without being able to speak or do simple tasks. You may not be able to fully comprehend such a life, but it became a reality to me and is for every stroke patient and survivor.

If you take a little time to understand what stroke patients go through, you will know that most of us end up losing our jobs. The stress of suffering and recovering is already a massive challenge, and losing our source of income multiplies that burden.

We are determined to get better but we often need your support to help us stay positive and be hopeful because it is difficult to pick ourselves back up, even more so if we find ourselves doing it alone. Even a simple message like telling us, "Don't quit!" works wonders.

We need you to help us turn our frustrations into hope. Be kind and patient with us because we have problems expressing ourselves or doing things on our own. We will experience forgetfulness, confusion, carelessness, and feelings of irritability. But we will get better over time. You need to be patient with us.

Slow But Steady

Every stroke patient's road to recovery will be slow but steady.  There will be numbers of stroke survivors that have residual disability. We never gave up and diligently worked on improving our speech, did regular physical exercise, learned, and focused on getting back the life we lived prior to stroke.

It will take a lot of work to adapt and cope with these residual deficits. Rehabilitation is an important part of care following a stroke.  This is the time when we need support to keep us active to improve outcomes following a stroke

There were times where it felt easier to just throw in the towel and give up when getting up in the morning felt too challenging and exhausting. It is during these times that we need your support more than ever.

We focus on the things we can control. We focus on

having a positive attitude towards everything happening to us. We keep ourselves busy and find fun things to do at home to keep our minds active.

Most of us, over time, will come to accept what we suffered or are suffering from a stroke. We focus on doing what we can in the present for a better future. Sadly, there will be many stroke patients still grasping and accepting that a stroke hit them.

We are at risk of many long-term complications associated with a stroke such as depression, joint pains due to prolonged immobilization; we also face the risk of clots in the veins of our legs, increased stiffness of our affected limbs, and constipation. Please be patient with us and help us manage these complications.

When someone suffers a stroke, please know that every second counts. It is always a medical emergency. The longer a stroke goes untreated, the greater the chance of lasting damage. Time lost is brain function lost.

Knowing that a stroke is a medical problem that can potentially be lethal is a start. We need to act F.A.S.T. We need you to know that you also need to act F.A.S.T.

F  is to check for face drooping

A  is to check for arm weakness

S  is to check for speech difficulty

T is to take note of the time the stroke occurred and call the emergency line.

During our recovery, getting support from family,

friends, and even support groups is also critical. Please support us to not miss therapy sessions and take prescribed medication regularly.

As a stroke survivor, we will see the risk of another stroke attack anytime, but every stroke patient works on reducing the chance of having another one. Your support and encouraging words go a long way for us on our journey to recovery.

The Pay-off

A motivation of love to all stroke patients and stroke survivors...

It was September 2019, almost four years since my first stroke attack, when I could finally say that I was 80% back to "normal." All these years, I have never given up on all my dreams and visualizing that I survived my multiple strokes.

Six years ago, I wanted to be an author and publish my own book. That dream finally came true in October 2020 as my book—Yes I Can—became a #1 bestselling book on Amazon. Nothing beats seeing my name on a book cover. It gives me fulfillment in life knowing that what I wrote will help change one person's life for the better.

Patience pays off. I believed that I would get better. I now believe that there was a silver lining to all that I suffered because it gave me opportunities for personal growth. It gave me a new direction in my life and my business by helping others, especially those who were affected economically. This is achieved with love.

My Vision To Empower Others

I came from a business background. I was able to resonate better with business owners. Having experienced how my stroke affected me economically, I decided to focus on helping other business owners acquire the skills and develop the systems to thrive in any economy.

I focus on being a "Rainmaker" in the small business world with my backend automation system which has helped automate 90% of the work that I do with my clients. The interesting part about using my platform and my A.C.C.—Attract, Connect, Convert—system is that it has helped my clients be "Rainmakers" themselves. It was no longer just about me; it was also about them helping themselves and others.

My fellow stroke fighters, believe in yourself that you have the "power" to empower others with what capabilities, skills, and knowledge you have. You are the same person before the stroke struck. Do not let anyone else tell you otherwise.

If you can empower just one person to change for a higher level, even with your current situation, you are actually a CHAMPION!

My Final Words

I am grateful that I was not paralysed by depression. Now, I am able to move around independently and talk to people, especially strangers, without stuttering. I am grateful that I am able to help my clients build their businesses. I am grateful that my business that had to stall due to my poor health is now slowly but surely coming back up again.

My journey has only just begun, and I have no intention of stopping any time soon. I was in your shoes a few years ago, but I chose to look for the arrival of my rainbow. I am grateful I have the support and love of my family.

8 December 2020, my beloved Mom suffered a stroke. She was a healthy and joyful person. She had no signs of being seriously ill and visited the doctor regularly for her checkups.

The stroke came suddenly and within days, we lost her. On 12 December 2020, she lost her battle to stroke and I lost my mom forever. To take it positively, due to her age and her it, I accepted the loss and grieved silently.

Stroke is real and it must be taken seriously. Taking action F.A.S.T. helps reduce the risk of long-term effects or lethal outcome.

I hope that by sharing my open letter of love, I can motivate other stroke patients and survivors to believe in themselves. Suffering from a stroke is not a handicap preventing you from making a difference in your own life and in others unless you let it.

I hope that sharing my story of being a stroke patient and surviving it, and also as a person who lost someone dear due to complications from a stroke, creates awareness that stroke is real.

I also hope that with my letter of love, there is now even greater awareness and understanding to the rest of the world of what stroke patients and survivors go through, and the type of support we need.

Giving up is not an option.

We have our dreams. Please hold our hands and help us push through our darkness. Help us catch our stars.

*"I focus on gratitude, wellness, and happiness. I grow from what I go through. I want my absence felt because I live for a cause!"*

With Love and Blessings. Be Happy, Be Safe, Be Healthy,

Nor Suhir

# Nor Suhir

Nor Suhir is #1 International Bestselling Author—Yes I Can—a stroke survivor, Certified Social Media Strategist, and Business Coach. She is also the President of the Hawkerentrepreneur Chapter at International Business Federation, Singapore, helping local food and beverage businesses digitalize, and recently launched her own Messenger automation application, ChatEngaged and her "Rainmaker" program—Attract, Connect, Convert (A.C.C.)

Contacts:

http://norsuhir.com

Email: nor@noamsinternational.com

ChatEngaged: http://chatengaged.com

Facebook: https://www.facebook.com/NorSuhir

Facebook Group: https://www.facebook.com/groups/701784610599373

Instagram: http://instagram.com/nor.suhir

# Dear Mum

You are the first woman I met with that strong scent of perfume that you wear. You've taught me a lot of life's lessons, like how to tie a shoe and even why I needed to get good grades at school. I watched you grow into a strong woman even though the years were not so kind to you, Mum. Yet you always looked on the bright side of life for everything.

We've had so many great holidays, like the time we went to England/Wales, and what did you do? You broke your ankle the first week we were there! I have never met a strong-willed woman like you, Mum. You have always been strong and fair with me, and even that time we were in England, you still persevered to make sure we all had a good time and a lovely Christmas together regardless of that broken ankle. Those were the days! They are the days that I will cherish always.

As I grew up over the years, I made some questionable choices and decisions, and most of the time, you tried to steer me towards a more sensible direction. I have always loved you for just being the mum you are.

The day I told you I was going into business for the first time, you looked at me with concern. You know that face that every mum pulls: happy and concerned at the same time. I know you told me, "What if it doesn't work out?" but I knew that it was what I wanted to do to change my life around and become the person I wanted to be. The love you had in your eyes for me said it all: "I love you, David. I don't want to see you disheartened in knowing it might all be for nothing."

I stood up for myself like that strong-willed woman you were many years ago in England. "I am doing it for me and my family," I said. I want to be that strong and fair person you were with me!

As years went by, after first chasing that dream of entrepreneurship, you saw me being that happy person I have always wanted to be. I love the work that I do, and I love knowing you are proud of me, too.

I have always loved you, Mum, for all those happy times and sorrows that we both endured together. My children have always brought happiness to you; know that they are in safe hands and have a childhood that almost any child would love to have. Your grandchildren have always been that rock. Their smiles, tears, and memories have brought this small family together.

The last few years have been a blessing and sadness at the same time. Our phone calls in the evening have brought us closer, and the times we were together around your house were the greatest moments of my life. The home I grew up in was the home any kid would wish they'd had. The year we had Christmas together, I dressed up as Santa for you and you let out the biggest laugh I have ever heard in all my years.

Seeing you laugh that day was like all the pain you had in your body disappeared for that brief moment. I am glad I saw you really smile, Mum, and I miss that laugh every day now.

The first time I saw you endure your first heart attack really scared me. Yes, I know you came around, and it was a blessing to know that you were still there for me. Those last few years were the best.

When I told you that I was writing my first book, you smiled at me! A smile knowing that you were proud of me. It was not until last year that God decided to take you away from me. You passed away during the night after another heart attack. I was glad that I was there with you during that early morning darkness.

I know I cry, Mum; it's because I still miss you and love you every day of my life. You weren't even there when my first book came out, but do you know what I did? I did my own little dedication to you during that book launch event, as I know deep down you have always been proud of me.

I love you, Mum!

You would not recognise what I have done now. I have grown much stronger as a person, even though we just went through the most terrible year of COVID. That strength nearly dissipated at one stage when we were locked down. On the day of the anniversary of your death, which in turn is also my birthday, I shed a single tear for you. Not just for the fact that you are gone, but for the fact that I know you would be proud of me and the choices I have made every single day since.

Looking back now, your strength and strong-willed attitude have been the cornerstone of my success. Thank you, Mum, and may your soul be at peace. I will soon see you again in the afterlife.

May my last words stay with you...

No good wishing you are around, but I know you are still with me in my heart, head, and soul!

I love you, Mum!

I will see you soon!

Lots of Love from David Vine, your loving son

# To my family,

There are so many things I want to say, but the first thing is the fact that I love every single one of you!

You might not think that I love you, but I do, yes. I have made questionable choices and decisions that none of you liked. Everything I have ever done was always because of the love that I have for you all. Some of you think that I'm a big meanie, a weird guy that dresses as Santa, doing University and writing books. And yes, those were *your* words.

My oath to every one of you is that even though my dreams are big and drive my ambition, my dreams still include each of you. Everything I have ever done is out of love and my way of putting food on the table. I have been well respected out of all my peers in the business world ... just some of you think that I am out of my league! We have all made mistakes, yes even me, but it's what we do with those mistakes and how we learn from them that matters.

Ever since life changed over the past few years, like the way society is changing because of COVID, and the family dynamics that constantly change, you might think that I am losing my mind when I am not. Family means everything to me, like the way I like to hold on to our family dinners, the obligations of Christmas you call it, or the holidays we have. It is my way of trying to hold on to those old lost memories of years gone by.

Life was so simple when you were all young. You could call it nostalgia because it is. I have always cherished those memories, and I miss them.

2020 has been a big year for all of us. One of you moved out of the home, another I hardly see because you are always out with your friends. The days when you were kids are nothing but memories now. I know you all are growing up. I accept that life is changing, and I hope for the fact that just one day you will be proud of the choices I have made.

My love for all of you will never change. I just hope your love for me will never change.

All I ask is that you please grow up and have your own memories, but don't grow apart!

We have a lot of great memories of our family holidays. Those were the days that we always looked forward to over the summer. My love will always be there, and my love as a father will never change. Please never doubt that.

The future is what you make of it. Make the right decisions, listen to some wise words from your father: life is not always easy. We make decisions that will change the course of our lives, and we must live by those choices no matter what we do. I have made mistakes, we all do, I just do not want to see you living by my mistakes.

 Stay strong, live your life, and always know that your father loves you! No matter what.

Lots of love from your father and loving husband, David

# David Vine

David Vine is a Business Owner, Self-Published Author, and Entrepreneur.

I was born in Brisbane/Australia and grew up in the suburbs of Logan City playing my computer games as a child. I have always been fascinated with technology, even at such a young age. You can say I have evolved with many different systems since the beginning with the original Atari and then moved on to a Commodore 63. My passion for writing and computers has grown, as I graduated from Kingston State High School 1993 and went to studying Diploma of Information Technology straight from high school.

I spent a few years working in different jobs, but they weren't challenging enough for me. Eventually, I went on to studying Diploma of Community Services at Logan TAFE and started to feel that urge in developing and helping people. Over the years, I became the family man with a lovely wife and three children which are now young adults and teenagers.

My entrepreneurial spirit did not start to kick in till I loved the idea of monetising what I already knew from teaching seniors from the computer club program that I helped start and instigated at the local school.

I love writing in all forms, from non-fiction business and empowerment type books, anthologies, and magazine contributions. Check out my works - https://www.facebook.com/david.vine.author

Email address: djvine@spin.net.au

# Get in Touch

Melissa Desveaux is an Author and Author Consultant, helping authors write and self-publish their own books.

If you've been thinking about writing your own book, get in touch with Melissa via:

Email - Melissa@melissadesveauxconsulting.com

Website - Melissadesveauxconsulting.com

Join the Get Published Program - get started by visiting the website.

Check out Melissa's other books

www.Melissadesveaux.com

Lightning Source UK Ltd.
Milton Keynes UK
UKHW050501020221
378086UK00001B/30